THE LONG ISLAND CITY POLICE DEPARTMENT

The Police of New York City

robert l. bryan

Published by robert l. bryan, 2023.

While every precaution has been taken in the preparation of this book, the publisher assumes no responsibility for errors or omissions, or for damages resulting from the use of the information contained herein.

THE LONG ISLAND CITY POLICE DEPARTMENT

First edition. July 26, 2023.

ISBN: 979-8223636199

Written by robert l. bryan.

For Meghan - always the angel on my shoulder.

INTRODUCTION:

Long Island City is the fastest growing neighborhood in the New York City borough of Queens. Throughout the 20th century LIC was best known for industrial commerce and production. This once industrial neighborhood is now an array of quaint residential blocks, such as the historical landmarked 45th Ave, new high-rise buildings, and old factory conversions. Many of those industrial brands have departed, and their legacies have been replaced with new landmarks of an up-and-coming cultural scene that has steadily developed in recent years. As Long Island City continues to gentrify, its decidedly industrial past keeps alive with former warehouse buildings and rail yards giving way to modern public green spaces, shops, and corner parks.

Vibrant eateries along Vernon Blvd. and cultural staples like MoMA PS1 and LIC Food & Flea provide entertainment options for both indoors and out. Gantry State Park and Hunter's Point Park South provide approximately 34 acres of green space along the East River with unmatched views of the Manhattan skyline.

But how did Long Island City blossom into the most vibrant neighborhood in the borough of Queens. How did it all begin? The answer was only a short distance away – on the other side of the East River.

On the cold, rainy evening of December 31, 1897, a throng of well-wishers gathered outside City Hall in Lower Manhattan to mark one of the most momentous occasions in the city's history: the consolidation of Manhattan, Queens, Brooklyn, the Bronx, and Staten Island into the Greater City of New York. Across the river, as the rain turned to snow, officials in Brooklyn were concluding a more somber ceremony——some called it a wake, to mark the end of Brooklyn's life as an independent city.

While the merger of Brooklyn and Manhattan was the big news, a third city lost its sovereignty that night: Long Island City, Queens. As midnight approached at the end of 1897, things in Long Island City were frantic. While the city's Board of Aldermen desperately tried to pass a last-minute funding bill to cover some of the city's mounting debt, someone pushed the arms on the clock in the council chamber back to give them more time. The city's mayor, Patrick "Battle Axe" Gleason (much more on him later), issued a rebuke to the council, noting:

I heartily congratulate the people of Long Island City that the Board of Alderman will soon be a thing of the past and that our financial affairs will be under the control and supervision of an honest and capable public officer under the new city government.

Long Island City had not paid its police officers in five months or its schoolteachers for seven months. This was not unexpected; almost from the city's founding a mere 28 years earlier, there had been accusations of graft and corruption. Outsiders knew the area mostly through the antics of Mayor Gleason, which ranged from colorful outbursts to acts of outright physical violence. As ceremonial cannons boomed and church bells tolled across the newly created five boroughs, there were probably many citizens of Long Island City who agreed with the mayor—an "honest and capable" government was going to be a nice change of pace.

Railroad transportation in the mid-1860s led to tremendous development in the municipalities of western Queens. The towns and villages began discussing the idea of sharing costs by consolidating into a city to be known as Long Island City.

The first inklings that there would eventually be a Long Island City came in 1865, when the Long Island City Star and Newtown Advertiser newspaper was founded, putting the name of the future city into the minds of local residents. The paper campaigned for the unification of western Queens, with Union College as a primary backer of the scheme.

The official beginning for the independent municipality of Long Island City began on February 16, 1869, the result of a public referendum in favor of consolidation. A home rule message and legislation were adopted by the LIC government which was forwarded to the New York State Legislature. The legislature passed the bill and Governor John T. Hoffman signed the bill into law.

The Governor was initially reluctant to sign the bill—perhaps because he'd already expended significant political capital in approving his friend William "Boss" Tweed's home-rule charter for New York City earlier that year—but on May 4, 1870, Hoffman approved the creation of Long Island City. Elections were held in early July, and on July 15, 1870, Abraham Ditmars was sworn in as the city's first mayor.

The new city was much larger than the Queens neighborhood of today. It had an area of 12 square miles and included Hunter's Point, Bowery Bay, Dutch Kills, Astoria, Ravenswood and Blissville, and a population of 31,000. The city was divided into 5 wards and was governed by a mayor, supervisor-at-large, and a board of aldermen.

The new city faced immediate challenges. Queens did not yet have running water or paved streets, and Long Island City found itself caught in the paradox of needing immediate improvements to lure residents and industries without the tax base to pay for such upgrades.

Luckily, at least one company saw the potential for growth in the new city: Steinway & Sons, the piano manufacturer, which had been established in a loft on Varick Street in 1853. In 1870, William Steinway began acquiring land in the newly created city, ultimately purchasing over four hundred acres of land with a frontage upon the East River and canal of about a mile. Steinway & Sons built a steam sawmill, iron and brass foundries, boiler and engine houses, a large building for the finishing of metal frames, storage sheds, drying kilns, docks, bulkhead wharves, a lumber basin, and in 1879, an immense structure to serve as a piano case factory.

A revised charter was passed in 1871 that called for a police force of 30 men, but the city did not have the revenue to hire them. No adequate fire department existed until 1893—five years before the city was subsumed into Greater New York City.

In the end, most of Long Island City's woes involved its politics, which were dirty from the start. In the second mayoral contest in 1872, Ditmars ran for reelection against the city clerk, Henry Debevoise, whose position put him in charge of overseeing elections. When Debevoise won, a group of citizens from Astoria sued for fraud, but a hung jury meant that Debevoise retained his position. He served on and off until 1880, when a new opponent, George Petry, again accused him of fraud. This time the charges stuck: Debevoise was stripped of his office and later fined over $100,000 for "misappropriating" city funds.

But those intrigues pale next to those of Patrick Gleason, who served as mayor from 1887 to 1892 and again as the city's final mayor from 1896 to 1897. He established the first successful streetcar company in Long Island City and entered politics in 1881 by joining the Long Island City Board of Alderman.

After a losing bid for mayor in 1883, he ran for alderman again in 1885, won—and then ran for mayor in 1886, winning that race as well. Since there was no law that said you couldn't serve as mayor and alderman at the same time, he held both positions, despite numerous entreaties for him to leave the board. His time in office was notable for "notorious corruption, crude vulgarity and flagrant use of patronage." [1]

But what about the police? Who was protecting the citizens in this growing city plagued with political corruption? Previous to the incorporation of the city the enforcement of the law was entrusted solely to constables supported by justices of the peace. There were four constables assigned to the area that would be within the municipal boundaries of the city -William Heaney, Thomas Darcy, Owen Slaven and Bernard Keagan.

Long Island City would have been larger, but Mayor Ditmars amended the city charter which resulted in the removal of Newtown from LIC. Newtown was able to levy their own taxes and maintained control of their schools and courts. Mayor Ditmars created a separate police force for LIC, which replaced the system of constables and justices of the peace that served the municipalities for decades as law enforcement.

It was obvious that the office of a town constable was not exempt from abuses and corruption considering that these four constables along with the three other constables covering the entire area of Newtown cost the public more than the whole police force of Long Island City after incorporation.

This old system, which had degenerated from a noble ancestry, was swept away upon the adoption of the charter of 1870. Acting under the police provision of the charter. Mayor Ditmars appointed Anthony S. Woods to the office of City Marshal, whose duties were both civil and criminal. Under the amended charter of 1871, Marshal Woods was promoted to the captaincy of the police department, the remaining members of the force being one sergeant and ten patrolmen. Though the charter provided for thirty patrolmen, it was found impracticable to put on a larger number of men, owing to inadequate appropriation of funds. The first Board of Police Commissioners, duly qualified under municipal law, was composed of John Bodine, Albert Gallatin Stevens and Joseph McLaughlin. Under successive administrations the police department performed its functions uneventfully for the most part, and without noteworthy interruption. Captain Woods remained in command of the force during the entire history of the city until the accession of Mayor Gleason to power in 1896, when he was arbitrarily deposed. At the end of its life, the Long Island City Police Department consisted of seventy-five patrolmen, one sergeant, one acting sergeant and a captain. The city always seemed to be in a never-ending fiscal crisis and the police exhibited an efficiency proportioned its limitations. In other words, there was never a time during the city's lifespan when the police department was adequately staffed. The number of patrolmen was insufficient to extend police protection over the various sections of the city. Even at the end of the city's independence, the one regular and one acting sergeant in each of the two precincts failed to provide adequate supervision for posts where twenty-four hours' service was required. The public interests suffered, not due to the efforts of the individual patrolmen and supervisors – there just were not enough of them and they worked under very challenging conditions.

An 1883 report prepared by Captain Woods on the condition of the LIC PD indicated that many deficiencies in the department existed. The captain concluded that there were insufficient supervisory personnel and patrolmen to adequately patrol the city; that the physical condition of both station-houses was "not fit to put human beings in;" that the station-houses were not connected by telephone; and that he had to pay for coal to heat the buildings from his own monies.

In that same year, a newly appointed Board of Police Commissioners was unable to meet the payroll and cut the number of officers from a force of eighty-three to seventy-three officers.

From the time Mayor Ditmars created the LIC PD in 1871, politics and the lack of revenue never permitted the force to efficiently police the jurisdiction. Over the next quarter of a century, the officers assigned to the two precinct stationhouses were subjected to management practices that broke their morale and caused consternation amongst taxpayers. Still, they went to work every day and performed like police officers all over the nation did, and still do.

It is rare that the history of a police department can be told through the prism of one man, but in the case of the Long Island City Police Department, the story of Anthony S. Woods is the story of the LIC PD. Captain Woods was there at the beginning and well past the consolidation. His story is an insight into the working conditions of the police department during the 28-year existence of Long Island City.

Long Island City Street Scene

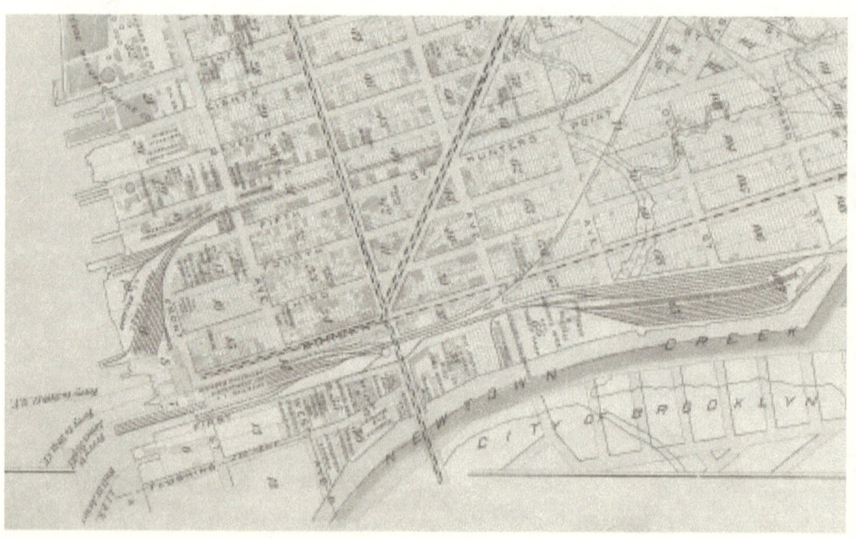

Late 1800s map of Long Island City

Main Street in Astoria

Vernon Boulevard in Long Island City

Long Island City Star Newspaper office

CAPTAIN WOODS

When Abraham Ditmars, the first mayor of Long Island City, set about the task of establishing the new city's infrastructure, he realized the police force would be a challenge. The city had been established in 1870, but the charter was amended in1871 to authorize the creation of a police force consisting of a chief, two sergeants, and 27 patrolmen. The headquarters for the new police force was established in a small wooden building on Broadway, in the Astoria section of the new city. The immediate problem for the mayor was that even though the charter allowed for 27 patrolmen, the city only had enough money to pay for ten. Who could he find to effectively manage and lead the police department of Long Island City with a third of the manpower it should have? The answer was simple – Anthony Woods.[2]

Anthony S. Woods was born in a house that stood at the corner of the Bowery and Third Street, in Manhattan, on October 3, 1827, and began his career in the paper trade. During the administrations of Presidents Pierce and Buchanan he was an attaché of the New York Customs House. He married Ms. Sarah M. Reynolds on November 25th, 1852, and they had eight children – four girls and two boys. In 1868 the family took up residence in Astoria.[3]

Mayor Ditmars appointed Woods City Marshal in 1870, and in 1871 when he needed someone to manage his newly formed, undersized police force with military discipline, he knew where to look. Woods served five years in the Grand Army of the Republic during the Civil War, retiring at the rank of Lieutenant Colonel.

At the time he assumed command of the police, the Hunter's Point section of Long Island City had the reputation for being a meeting place for many thieves and low lives. The job for the ten original patrolmen involved long hours and many hazards and dangers. The only way to keep them operating with any efficiency was to treat them as a military body. Woods was directed by the Board of Police Commissioners to drill the patrolmen in military tactics, and the manual of arms. Mayor Ditmars secured from the State officials thirty new rifles with bayonets and other accoutrements, and the wooden headquarters building soon became a small arsenal. The guns were inspected and polished regularly and each man on the force had a weapon to care for. In time the force was increased to the charter limit, and drills were held regularly. Sometimes the company of bluecoats would march across country to Blissville and drill in the big hall attached to Supervisor Joe McLoughlin's hotel, on Greenpoint Avenue. Other places were used for drilling and the marches were made an opportunity to explain to the men the features of skirmishing and the advantage of trees and shrubbery as screens from an enemy.

The drills were usually witnessed by crowds of spectators. The police were put through all the evolutions and each man knew his place and what was expected of him. The constant drilling kept up the interest of the men and made them very efficient and self-reliant. The small force was able to cover a great deal of territory and as each man was kept in prime condition by regular exercise, they were well able to handle crowds and toughs.[4]

As head of the Long Island City Police, Woods was given the rank of Captain. While drilling his men in military tactics, perhaps Woods should have spent some time on some basic detective instruction. In 1872 there was a very strange case involving captain Woods, himself, that called into question the lack of very basic investigative skills.

Captain Woods was reported missing over a period of two days. He had visited New York and was last seen on Park Row, about four o'clock in the afternoon. He had never been known to stay away from home for a single night, or to have tasted a drop of liquor and the entire police force was mobilized to find him.[5] As day two passed without any word on Captain Woods, his wife was in a state of mind bordering on insanity, as she had never known her husband to remain away for a single night since the Civil War. The Long Island City Policemen fanned out across Manhattan, visiting all the hospitals and public places in their unsuccessful search. More and more it was feared that Captain Woods had become the victim of foul play.[6] Then, suddenly, the search was over. Captain Woods was found to be sick in bed in his home in Astoria. How was this possible? Who knows? I would hope his wife and the police force would have checked the bed in his home before searching all over Manhattan.[7]

The story of the Long Island City Police department is closely entwined with the story of Captain Woods. After all, Woods was around from the birth of the city right up until it breathed its last breath at the Consolidation of 1898. Of course, Woods was not leading the police force for the entire 28-year period. During several of those years he was either suspended or dismissed from the force, and that's what makes his story so interesting. The turbulent relationship Woods had with the mayors, police commissioners, and other politicians contained a common thread – pool selling.

When I first read the term "pool-selling," I envisioned the time many years ago when I was inside a showroom listening to a fast talking salesman attempt to sell me a swimming pool that was too expensive for my budget and too big for my backyard. Although that shyster was unethical, there was nothing illegal about his tactics, so that could not be the "pool-selling" causing so many problems in Long Island City in the late 19th century.

In American cities in the 1800s there were hundreds of illicit gambling rackets, called poolrooms, usually alongside the seediest taverns and brothels. In New York, one could find the poolrooms filled mostly with recently arrived Irish immigrants betting on horseracing. The activity was called pool-selling because the participants were betting into a pool. For example, six horses named A, B, C, D, E, and F are entered into a race. Individuals who want to wager on the winner of the race approach the operator inside the poolroom. The wagering individual buys one ticket for $5 on horse C. The operator makes out a ticket indicating the amount wagered and the horse it was wagered on. The board is then adjusted to display how many tickets have been sold for each horse and is updated continuously. Ticket sales end right as the race begins. In this example 100 tickets, worth $5 each, have been sold. There were 10 tickets sold for horse A, 20 for B, 25 for C, 5 for D, 10 for E, and 30 for F. All told there is $500 in the pool of bets. The operators would then take their commission, which was originally 10%. So, there is now $450 to be distributed to the individuals holding winning tickets. If horse A wins, each ticket for horse A pays $45; if horse B wins, each ticket pays $22.50; if horse C wins, each ticket pays $18, and so on. Parimutuel wagering found immediate success in America.

In 1879 Manhattan began to crack down on gambling activities, including the poolrooms. It didn't take long for the proprietors of these operations to realize they had fertile ground waiting across the river in Long Island City. The money generated by these gambling dens constituted one of the primary areas of corruption within the Long Island City government. It wasn't just a simple case, however, of politicians greedily lining their pockets. These poolrooms brought thousands of people to Long Island City, and these people did not limit their spending to gambling activities. They also injected much needed cash into the other businesses in the city, cash that was desperately needed.

Captain Woods found himself caught in the middle between the forces that wanted to rid Long Island City of the poolrooms, and those who wanted to let the activity continue, whether it was in the interests of the city or themselves.

Public sentiment was significantly against the settlement of the pool sellers in Long Island City, adjacent to the ferries. These establishments had been running successfully for over a month and were daily visited by a thousand or more people. There were three main proprietors - Harry Hill, William Lovell, and Kelly & Bliss, who ran the largest operation.

It was thought that the grand jury would indict them, but it did not because the District Attorney had no evidence to present. A one-armed man representing the New York Society for the Suppression of Crime was at the courthouse to give testimony, but before he could get to the grand jury room the spies of the pool men made loud threats against him, causing him to leave through fear of violence. The grand jury said more evidence was coming and the pool men would likely be indicted.

It was said that an effort would be made to indict the Police Commissioners for failing to suppress the illegal businesses, so the Commissioners decided to take action forthwith. They passed a resolution in June of 1879 ordering Captain Woods to stop the businesses. The Captain proceeded in a peculiar way. Instead of raiding the places he meekly presented himself before the judge and asked for warrants of arrest for Hill, Kelly, Bliss, and Lovell. Then he brought Kelly, Bliss and Lovell before the judge where they pled not guilty while the games were in full blast. Hill was not found.

The whole thing seemed to be well understood between the gamblers and the police. Some of the city officials were interested in the games. The object seemed to be to continue the preliminary examination until after the adjournment of the Court of Sessions in hopes that the grand jury would not meddle with the matter. The people wanted the businesses closed but too many people were making money – the businesses themselves and the saloons and other stores in the area where the people were flocking to. Many politicians were getting their share, so the common belief was that the pool rooms had the protection of the police and the commissioners.[8]

In the meantime, Captain Woods had other issues to worry about – issues regarding his own safety. On a Monday night Philip Ahearn, 19 years old, went into Ring's Saloon, at Dutch Kills, and with a stone, which he carried in his hand, knocked Mr. Ring senseless. Some men rushed out of the barroom as Captain Woods hurried in, to find Ahearn with a knife drawn. The Captain reached out to clutch him, and Ahearn made a lunge at him with the knife, making an incision across the back of his hand. In the struggle which ensued the Captain got possession of the knife, and Ahearn got away with the Captain's club, but was overtaken before he had gone far.[9]

In a case that bears a striking resemblance to the controversy surrounding today's bail reform laws, the same Philip Ahearn was arrested two months later for attempting to take the life of John Malay with a knife. After his arrest for attempting to kill Police Captain Woods, he was believed to be insane and released.[10]

A new Police Board took office in 1882 and held their first meeting in January. Captain Woods presented a statement showing the condition of the department. The statement set forth that the department was in a very unsatisfactory condition. There should have been four sergeants instead of two. There were only six posts in the city whereas there should have been at least 19 which would require 70 patrolmen instead of 21, the present number. No patrol duty was done between the hours of 8 AM and 2 PM. Both station houses were unfit to be used for police purposes. The cells at the second precinct station house were not fit to put human beings in. The station houses should have been connected by telephone, and the same manner of communication should have been established between the waterworks and the Brooklyn Police Headquarters. The department was without coal, and the last ton purchased Woods had to pay out of his own pocket, as the local coal dealers refused to sell the city any more coal on credit. Not a word was mentioned about the poolrooms.[11]

Pool-selling continued to operate openly in Long Island City. Early in 1882 Governor Cornell sent a semi-mandatory letter to District Attorney Downing, who, at the head of a squad of police, raided the poolrooms and made some arrests of clerks who were fined $75, while the owners were not charged.

Downing received no credit for this aggressive move because for about two years he had stood callous against public sentiment and the appeals of the newspapers during which time gambling prospered. When, therefore, pool-selling was renewed several weeks after the raid, no one was surprised.

Public pressure motivated the Police Board to hold a special meeting and they passed several resolutions condemning the pool-selling establishments. Captain Woods got his men ready to make a raid but was prevented by a resolution of the Police Board, adopted a half hour before the raid, which forbade any interference with the gambling.

Resolved: That the captain be directed not to interfere with any parties said to be selling or engaged in selling pools until further orders from this board and in the meantime to procure all the evidence within his reach of a positive nature that the State law on gambling is being violated.

One of the commissioners, Mr. Williams, stated to a reporter that he was not familiar with the law regarding these places, and he was not fully informed of the powers of the commissioners in these premises. He declared emphatically if he found any games of red and black or faro in progress, he would order the arrest of the offenders immediately.[12]

Not many people believed the Captain. Pool-selling on horse races and other sports was now openly being carried on in Long Island City, and hundreds of men floated from place to place every afternoon. It was taken for granted by the pool-sellers that they were not to be interfered with anymore.[13]

Therefore, it was a surprise to many to see Captain Woods with a squad of his men march from the station house to the poolrooms at about 9 AM. Whether it was with or without the blessing of the Police Commissioners on July 2nd Captain Woods and 14 men raided the poolrooms that had been running unmolested for months.[14]

Policemen were stationed at the entrance to each poolroom. The rooms were all in buildings on the same block and when the police activity was observed, many believed a genuine raid was being made and much excitement prevailed in the neighborhood. When Captain Woods and his troops burst in there were only a few clerks in the rooms, which should not have been a surprise since the poolrooms did not open until the afternoon.

No attempt was made to arrest anyone, and the clerks remained in possession of the rooms, keeping the doors closed. Captain Woods and his men remained on duty at the rooms until 1 PM when they suddenly withdrew. About this time the patrons of the rooms began to arrive and soon a brisk business was being done in each place.

When questioned, Captain Woods said, "I merely placed men at each place to find out if pools were being sold."

He did not explain, however, how his men could accomplish such a task while the doors were closed. Only one story was going around the city, and that was to the effect that the pool-sellers had been paying a weekly "boodle", and that the prior week the money had been paid as usual but did not pass through the proper channel, which resulted in the pool-sellers being threatened with a police raid. When they saw the police surrounding their places the story went that the proprietors had to reach a settlement with certain politicians.[15]

The public pressure to close the poolrooms continued, and Captain Woods again proposed raiding the establishments, but was prevented by a resolution passed by the Police Commissioners. Following this came a declaration by District Attorney Downing stating that he was not a detective and did not propose to repeat his earlier raid. Accordingly, the pool-sellers felt secure in running their operations.

The pool-sellers felt they were solidly established, and it seemed so until suddenly, on July 8th at about 8 AM Captain Woods and eight men attracted attention by halting in front of Kelly & Bliss poolroom. The Captain deployed his men and assigned them in two to do duty at each of the pool rooms, with instructions to allow no one to enter, and if the doors were thrown open to arrest those inside. The Captain at the same time gave notice to the persons in charge of the rooms that no business would be allowed. The result was a big commotion with men inside the rooms running here and there trying to notify their superiors of the raid. At about noon, when the business of the poolrooms normally began, the police stole quietly away, the poolroom doors were thrown open for the reception of the usual thousands of persons.[16]

Just as the story of the Long Island City Police Department could not be told without Captain Woods, the Story of the city would never be complete without Patrick Gleason. Paddy "Battle Ax" Gleason, was the most important political figure during the short life of Long Island City in both a positive and negative sense. There will be much more on Gleason later, but in 1882 it was Alderman Gleason who was loud in denouncing the action of the police and characterized the poolroom situation as an official blackmail. This sentiment also seemed to be the common opinion among the people, but the question uppermost was who was responsible for the placing and withdrawing the police. Alderman Gleason said he would make an effort to find out.

At the meeting of the Board of Alderman a committee of investigation was appointed. The committee held two sessions, but no light was shed on the peculiar action of the police. It was said by an alderman that a person holding a city office had been collecting a boodle and disposing of it on the division and silence plan, meaning that he distributed the payoff to the politicians who were supposed to receive a share and then kept silent. The alderman said he knew where the swag went, and that he would finally expose the parties. He was not opposed to pool-selling but insisted that if the business was to continue it should not pay bribe money, and the police should not be used to aid in such corruption.

Several days earlier a policeman made eight arrests of pool-sellers and arraigned the parties before Judge Delahanty, who discharged the defendants and reprimanded the officer.[17]

On July 20th the Police Commissioners instructed Captain Woods to immediately close the poolrooms.[18] So, when Police Commissioner Williams returned home after several days absent from the city he expressed surprise that the pool-sellers had not been expelled from the city in compliance with the order of the Police Board. He said that if Captain Woods would not do his duty he would have to be dismissed.[19]

The threat of termination must have motivated Captain Woods to action, but he apparently wanted some protection for himself, which resulted in another attempt to close the poolrooms at Hunter's Point ending in a farce.

Before initiating the raid, Captain Woods went to City Hall to receive a certified copy of the resolution passed by the Police Commissioners instructing him to close the poolrooms and arrest any person found selling pools in Long Island City. He was informed by City Clerk Moran, who was also clerk to the Police Commissioners, that there had been no meeting of the board, and that the resolution was not worth the paper it was written on.[20]

For more than two months the Police Commissioners had been meeting and passing resolutions directing Captain Woods to break up the poolrooms and other gambling houses, but he had done nothing to that end and public feeling in the matter was running high. Commissioner Williams sent his resignation to Mayor Debevoise but was never notified of its acceptance by the Mayor, so he continued to act officially. On the evening of the meeting where the last resolution directing Woods to close the poolrooms had been ratified, Commissioner McGarry was out of town, so it was Commissioners Armstrong and Williams who passed the resolution. The reason City Clerk Moran had told Woods the resolution wasn't worth the paper it was written on was because the Mayor had accepted Williams' resignation prior to the passage of the resolution. Therefore, Williams was not a Commissioner, and one Commissioner could not pass a resolution. Therefore, there was no raid, nor did it seem that there was likely to be one.[21]

The attempt to have the police close the poolrooms had resulted in total failure. Ex-Commissioner Williams said the mayor did not accept his resignation when he presented it but Mayor Debevoise denied that. In fact, the Mayor had seen Captain Woods shortly after Williams submitted his resignation and he told Woods the resignation had been accepted. If that was true, Woods knew the resolution passed by the Commissioners was not proper. Why didn't he say anything at the meeting?[22]

The new Police Board of President McGarry, and Commissioners Tier and Clark met in August, and there was a strong feeling that they would address the pool-selling issue. Instead, Captain Woods provided a generic report about the state of the Long Island City Police Department detailing the strength of the department to be 1 captain, 2 sergeants and 29 patrolmen. He also reported on the deplorable condition of the station house cells, but not one word was spoken regarding the pool-selling establishments.[23]

The Police Commissioners were to meet on September 27th to address the poolroom problem, but they did not have a quorum with Commissioner Tier traveling to Mineola to attend the Queens County Fair. Captain Woods continued to insist he would not interfere unless he received written orders from his superior officers.[24]

On October 1st the Police Commissioners met and passed a resolution directing Captain Woods to close the poolrooms immediately. The Captain refused, however, stating that he had not received a copy of the resolution, but Commissioner Tier said he saw a copy of the resolution placed into the Captain's hand when the resolution was passed. It was expected that the raid would take place on the 4th, but gambling proceeded without interruption into the evening of the 3rd.

Before the raid could be organized, word was privately communicated to the pool-sellers of the Commissioner's intention to raid them, so they shut down operations on their own. Alderman Gleason was credited with finally getting the Commissioners to pass the resolution because he threatened to go to the grand jury to have them indicted for dereliction of duty.[25]

The next day the Commissioners provided another copy of their resolution to Captain Woods and directed him to ensure the pool-seller did not open. At this time Captain Woods produced written orders from the Mayor countermanding the orders of the Commissioners. The Commissioners told Woods if he did not obey their orders he would be dismissed. Commissioners Tier and McGarry went to see the mayor at his residence at Blissville and told him they had ordered the poolrooms closed and that if he interfered, they would immediately resign. The mayor did not attempt to interfere after that.[26]

The pool sellers opened up business again on October 6th without any interference from the police. Several officers were on duty in the vicinity of the rooms, where they could hear the cry of the auctioneer as he sold first and second choice and the field on each race. The police concerned themselves only in keeping the crowds off the sidewalks.

The poolroom issue had become a question of authority between the Mayor and the Commissioners, and Mayor Debevoise was not about to have his Police Board threaten to resign, so he removed Commissioner McGarry and replaced him with Commissioner Carroll. Within an hour of the change every gambling house in the city was running. Commissioner Tier was threatened with the ax unless he acquiesced to the mayor's wishes.

On January 31, 1883, the new Police Board of Long Island City issued an order to Sergeant James McManus of the Second Precinct, ordering him to take command of the force and to notify Captain Woods and nine other members of the department that they were suspended. The order also set forth that the suspended members should turn in their department equipment. The suspended men believed they were being dismissed from the force, but the Commissioners said the reduction was necessary on account of the crippled financial condition of Long Island City. They acted under the amended charter which gave the Commissioners power to suspend any member of the force at any time when such suspension was rendered necessary on account of the condition of the city's finances. Captain Woods was very distressed when informed of his suspension in the presence of his men. He said he did not think he should deliver up his shield until he had consulted with a lawyer.[27]

Captain Woods circulated a petition requesting the Board of Aldermen to secure the passage of an act repealing the power of the Commissioners to suspend or remove a police officer.[28] Two weeks later Captain Woods and the other suspended members still refused to surrender their shields, and on February 16th they appeared in full uniform at a hearing to consider their case. Counselor Howe appeared on behalf of Woods and the suspended men, and he talked so roughly that one Commissioner almost had him ejected from the building.[29]

On May 15th Captain Woods demanded through the New York State Supreme Court his restoration to duty and back pay amounting to $600. He claimed that he was dismissed without charges, but the Commissioners responded that they had the power to suspend when they had no money to pay police salaries. They also noted that Woods still had possession of department property he had not turned in. The motion was denied.[30] In June, the Commissioners went one step further, Captain Woods had still not returned his department property so they charged him with misappropriating $114. [31]

In July of 1884 Captain Woods won a moral victory in the fight to get his job back. The general Term of the Supreme Court ordered the Board of Police Commissioners to reinstate him. The Board refused to obey the order of the court, so Woods moved to have the Board punished for contempt of court. The Police Commissioners said there was no money to pay his salary, and that the Board had passed a resolution dismissing Woods until there should be sufficient money to meet the expense of a captain's salary. The victory was moral because the Court drew a distinction between their order of reinstatement and the city's ability to pay the salary, ruling they were two separate issues. Captain Woods continued in his suspended state.[32]

In 1885 Captain Woods was still without a job, but he was forging relationships with friends who would be instrumental to his future return. His most important was with Patrick Gleason, who was now a former Alderman after losing an election. Joseph McLaughlin had also just lost an election. The former City Supervisor had been beaten by George Smith, with Alderman Gleason and Captain Woods playing a vocal role in supporting Smith. On this January evening, Woods and Gleason were out to dinner together, and they had chosen to dine in a hotel in Blissville opposite the new entrance to Calvary Cemetery. This hotel just happened to be owned by Joseph McLaughlin.

In the dining room of the hotel, McLaughlin ended up sitting at a table near Woods and Gleason. It didn't take long for either his rage or alcohol consumption to rise, or perhaps it was a combination of the two. McLaughlin began with some disparaging remarks to Captain Woods about the previous election. The Captain excused himself to the barroom in an attempt to diffuse the situation. McLaughlin picked up a heavy glass salt cellar from the table and followed Woods into the barroom. By the way, a salt cellar was a type of dish used to dispense salt in 19th century restaurants.

Without saying a word McLaughlin hurled the salt cellar at Woods' head, but it missed the Captain and struck Augustus Hetner, the bartender. Hetner was struck over the left eye, cutting him badly.

McLaughlin followed up by punching Woods in the mouth, cutting his lip and causing some blood to flow. Several men in the barroom got between the two before Woods could return the blow.

The Captain made a brief attempt to go after McLaughlin, but quickly regained his composure and left the hotel.

Just then, Patrick Gleason, who did not realize a fight had started, entered the barroom and was immediately assailed by Mclaughlin with a diatribe of curses. The epithets angered Gleason so much, he made a dash for McLaughlin but was restrained, and by the advice of friends he headed off in the direction of the hotel barber shop, intending to go to his office in an adjacent building.

McLaughlin began a pursuit of Gleason and passed Justice Stephen Kavanaugh as the justice was on his way to the dining room. Kavanaugh observed McLaughlin pull a pistol from his pocket and he quickly wrenched it from McLaughlin's hand, an action for which Kavanaugh received a kick in the stomach so severe that he fainted and had to be revived with brandy and water.

By the time McLaughlin got into the barber shop Gleason was already gone, but that didn't stop him from trying to fight someone. He took off almost all his clothes and challenged any man in the city friendly with Gleason to a fight. Eventually, some of McLaughlin's friends got him dressed and took him home.

Whether he realized it at the time or not, the punch in the mouth he received was very fortunate for Captain Woods. It only served to bring him even closer to Paddy Gleason, a friendship that would prove very important in the not too distant future.[33]

Patrick Gleason assumed the office of Mayor of Long Island City in 1887. What Marc Antony said about Julius Caesar in his famous play about the Roman dictator, "The evil that men do lives after them; The good is oft interred with their bones," was also true about Long Island City's legendary Irish mayor Paddy Battle Axe Gleason. A deeply polarizing figure, Gleason was attacked by his enemies for his alleged corruption, buffoonery, and brawling. Gleason, however, was also adored by Long Island City's Irish working class and especially its school children. Gleason remains one of the most colorful and charismatic figures in New York City history, but also one of the most reviled and misunderstood.

Gleason arrived in New York in 1862 following four of his brothers who would serve in the Union Army. Amazingly, his twin brother Phillip would serve in the Confederate Cavalry in an army fighting his twin and four siblings. Gleason enlisted and soon transferred to the New York 63rd Regiment, where his brother John was an officer of legendary bravery who had been recruited by Bishop John Hughes of New York City on behalf of Governor Edwin D. Morgan to fight for the Union cause during the Civil War

Patrick never won medals like his brother but made a unique claim. Gleason told a story of digging a trench not far from Washington D.C. while serving in the Army of the Potomac under General McClellan. A shadow fell over the trench and as he looked up, he saw a tall lanky fellow standing above and gazing down at him. "That's a pretty tattered pair of breeches you have on," said the tall man. Gleason agreed, but replied, "Uncle Sam seems short of trousers for us these days." Lincoln asked him his name and company and Gleason returned to his digging. A few days later, Gleason's captain summoned him to his tent and then informed him that he had a package from the White House. When Gleason opened the package, he found a pair of breeches with a note from Lincoln saying, "I think that you and I are of the same build, Private Gleason. When I got home, I found this pair of trousers. They have been worn a bit, but they are better than the ones that you have. I hope they fit." Abraham Lincoln.

After the war. Patrick returned to New York where he ran a distillery in Flushing and told stories for years about how he hid his profits from snooping government inspectors. Borrowing money to sail to California, Gleason found work in a San Francisco distillery whose owner paid him $5,000 to reveal his distilling secrets. Speculating in the stock market, Gleason amassed $30,000, a fortune at the time and returned to New York a wealthy man.

Gleason opened a tavern in Williamsburg, Brooklyn, where in 1872 he ran unsuccessfully as a Democrat for New York State Assembly. Gleason always claimed he received the most votes and was cheated out of his victory. After his defeat, Gleason moved across Newtown Creek into Queens, where he settled in the rapidly growing waterfront community of Long Island City. Gleason established a horse carriage line for families visiting their dead relatives nearby in Calvary Cemetery in 1874, making it the first trolley line on Long Island outside of Brooklyn.

Long Island City was already infamous for corrupt politics. Its mayor, Henry S. Debevoise, was removed from office for his part in a money-laundering scheme, and in 1882, running as a reformer, Gleason won election as an alderman. That same year proved to be one of the most fateful in the history of Long Island City. New York City, in a rare burst of municipal virtue, had outlawed gambling and bookmaking, and to stay in business bookies moved to pool halls and saloons in Long Island City, where they were only a ferry ride away from their customers and the police could be bribed to turn a blind eye. Faro and roulette tables quickly began to appear, and Gleason soon opened a gambling house conveniently near the waterfront.

The Democrats nominated Gleason to run for Mayor by the Democrats, but then tragedy struck when his wife died, leaving Gleason a widower with a four-month-old daughter. Gleason was so shaken by the tragic death of his wife that he left politics, but not for long. In the next Aldermanic election of 1885 Gleason was elected and in November 1886, he ran for mayor as an independent without being nominated by the Regular Democrats or Independent Democrats, running against incumbent George Petry. He won 1436 votes to Petry's 1258 thanks to the vote of the working-class Irish. Gleason now occupied two offices at once: alderman and mayor; when asked to resign his council seat he refused on the grounds that there was no statute in the City Charter forbidding dual office holding which was true and Gleason's dual status gave him unique power; he could act as a legislator and then pass or veto his own legislation.

Gleason's popularity stemmed in part from his role as a champion of the oppressed. He had the fare on the ferry from Manhattan lowered to 3 cents. He attacked "soulless" polluting corporations like Standard Oil and fought to have some of their refineries in LIC removed. He once attended a meeting of the City Council and Standard Oil paid several goons to intimidate him from speaking. Before rising to speak he glared at the thugs and asked whether anyone present wanted a run-in. No one dared challenge him and after making a speech attacking Standard Oil his listeners cheered.

One of Gleason's first official acts as Mayor was to reinstate captain Woods as Chief of Police. Captain Woods was not back on the job long before he became embroiled in a controversy that was both business and personal.

On July 4th 1887 18-year old Gussie Werner attended a holiday picnic. The next day she was found unconscious in the kitchen of the home where she worked and was thought to have been overcome by the heat. She recovered during the afternoon and appeared to be as strong as ever. At approximately 6 PM she was sent to the meat market, where she made her purchases, paid the bill and started for home with the goods. That was the last seen of her. A very quiet unsuccessful search was conducted, and after fourteen days the missing person case was finally entered into the blotter of the Long Island City Police Department. The girl was never found, and it was believed that her mind became affected and that she wandered near the river, fell in and drowned.

Why did it take so long for this disappearance to become an official police case? Perhaps it was because Gussie Werner worked in the home of captain Woods.[34] Woods was roundly condemned for keeping the disappearance of his servant hidden for so long. Some reporters felt her disappearance was clearly due to a mental condition, and for that reason, if for no other, the police should have promptly sent out an alarm. That she worked for Captain Woods gave him no license to treat her case differently from any other. One reporter then took a swipe at the police by stating that Long Island City was deficient in a good many things, but in none more so than intelligent police service.[35]

The police of Long Island City still seemed to be as ignorant as ever to the subject of pool-selling and bookmaking at Mike Kearney's Cockpit in Blissville, close to Calvary Cemetery. Groups of men having a password went in and out while two officers stood staring blankly at the building

"I don't know what those men are going in there for," Said one of the policemen. "I can see no harm in it. They are orderly enough."

In a large room, having a gallery at one end and ornamented with two wooden roosters holding a banner inscribed, "Welcome," two bookmakers were at work, and at a long table, combination bets were made. The gambling had been going on for two weeks without interference from the police, although Mayor Gleason and Captain Woods both declared that neither bookmaking nor pool-selling would be tolerated.[36]

On August 27th Mayor Gleason and Captain Woods answered their critics with a raid on the Blissville poolroom. The operation was carried out without the slightest leak, which was evidenced by the 57 arrests made, including a City Alderman. As usual, however, Mayor Gleason employed some questionable legal tactics. Gleason acted as a magistrate and signed the warrants for the raid himself for fear of leaking the intent of the raid by seeking out a local magistrate for the warrants.[37]

The relationship between Gleason and Woods remained solid. During September, Gleason attended a meeting with the Water Department. An accountant named Martin accused the Mayor of inconsistent behavior in that as Alderman he had demanded an investigation of the department accounts, and now as Mayor he seemed to be trying to avoid the same type of investigation. Martin had not finished his speech before Gleason turned to Captain Woods and said, "Put this fellow out."

Captain Woods elevated his club and pointed it in the direction of the exit. "Git!" the Captain ordered.

Martin's speech was over.[38]

It wasn't long before a falling out occurred between Mayor Gleason and Captain Woods. The exact reason for the animosity was not known. Perhaps it was the Mayor's disregard for the law when it came to forwarding his agenda, whether it be for the benefit of the people or himself.

A good starting point for the animosity may well have been June 6, 1888. Mayor Gleason had an ongoing feud with the Long Island railroad, and on that day, he ordered Captain Woods to arrest Long Island Railroad employees who were unloading express wagons at the offices on Borden Avenue for obstructing the public streets. This may seem like a very routine assignment, but the first man arrested was Anthony Woods, the son of Captain Woods. The younger Woods was in charge of the LIRR express offices and was arrested with another LIRR employee. Both were paroled by the mayor.[39]

Gleason's most memorable moment with the railroad, and likely as Mayor occurred a little more than a month later. These were the days before Penn Station existed and Long Island City had become the hub for the Long Island Railroad. It was the terminal for trains coming from eastern Long Island as well as the connection to their ferries to Manhattan. For several years, first Alderman Gleason and then Mayor Gleason steamed as he watched what he considered an attempt by the LIRR to take over Long Island City with all their tracks and structures infringing on the city streets and causing obstructions and hazards to the public.

On July 26th, the Long Island City Commissioner of Public Works, Patrick Harrigan was walking along Front Street when he came upon a newly erected fence and gate by an LIRR ticket booth. Harrigan attempted to pass through the gate but was prevented by railroad guards. He told the guards they were obstructing a public highway, but they refused to move. Harrigan made an about face and went directly to the Mayor's office. That was the final straw.

The following day around 2 PM an odd army of police, city laborers and members of the public assembled behind their general, Mayor Patrick Gleason. Ten laborers had gathered in a wagon load of crowbars, sledgehammers, saws, and axes. Gleason directed the weapons distributed amongst his troops. He shouted "Are you ready boys?" and then he gave the order to charge.

The Long Island City Police formed a perimeter around the areas of battle to prevent interference while Gleason and his troops went to work along Front Street tearing down LIRR fences, sheds, and ticket booths. All the LIRR employees fled, and Gleason provided an inspiration for his men with his work with an ax. At the end of the raid when all the railroad fences and structures were gone, the mayor had a new nickname. Paddy "Battle Ax" Gleason addressed a group of reporters and declared, "The railroad will not infringe upon the rights of the people of this city while I am mayor."[40]

The poolrooms of Long Island City were like boomerangs – they kept coming back. A year after the successful raid on Mike Kearney's Blissville establishment, another poolroom at the exact same location was ready to open for business. For two weeks the proprietor was making preparations for the grand opening, but unbeknownst to him Mayor Gleason had planted an undercover detective inside the establishment.

It was about 1 PM on March 30, 1889, when crowds of men had gathered at the new poolroom. A message was received from the detective that business had begun, and crowds were pouring in over the Blissville Bridge. James Davren was a member of the Board of Assessors and he was also an undertaker. When the four coaches were seen leaving the Davren's livery stable they appeared to be nothing more than a funeral procession. But there was no funeral. The carriages proceeded to the German settlement in Astoria and took in sixteen policemen along with Captain Woods and Sergeant Cosgrove. When the carriages reached Calvary Cemetery, they fell in behind a real funeral procession and approached the poolroom without arousing the slightest suspicion. There was no concern when the carriages stopped. The first floor of the poolroom was a saloon, and it was custom for the drivers of coaches at funerals to stop to allow mourners to drink after the burial. Some of the policemen took up positions by the doors while the majority of the squad rushed up to the gambling rooms on the second floor. The police moved so rapidly they had established complete control of the building before a single man could escape. 115 arrests were made including Owen Kavanaugh, the Chief of the Rockaway Beach Police Department.

Mayor Gleason sat as judge after the arrests and had the culprits brought before him one by one. The majority were discharged and the few on whom fines were imposed paid the money willingly and departed. The fines were very light, ranging from $1 to $5.[41]

An example to how low the relationship between the Mayor and Captain Woods had sunk occurred during the processing of the arrests. When the case against Kearney, the proprietor of the poolroom was called, Assistant District Attorney Cornelius was called to a room by Mayor Gleason for a private consultation. Captain Woods followed Cornelius into the room with two men in civilian attire.

"Who are these men?" Mayor Gleason asked.

"They are witnesses," Woods replied.

"Now you lie," Gleason declared, "and you get out of here, you dirty big loafer," he said to Woods.

Captain Woods stormed out of the room without a word.[42]

As time went on Captain Woods' relationship with Mayor Gleason continued to deteriorate, but in 1891 he also began having strained relations with the police officers. The issue developed when two officers refused orders that they claimed were given by Captain Woods in violation of Long Island City Police regulations. Patrolmen worked 12-hour shifts. The first 6-hours were on patrol and the second 12-hours in reserve. During the reserve time the officers were permitted to go to bed in the station house and sleep.

On two successive evenings officers contested the orders given in relation to the regulation. On the first night, Patrolman Thomas Mulligan entered the station house after his 6-hours on patrol. The police department was very short staffed, so Sergeant Roulette directed Mulligan to remain on patrol duty by direction of Captain Woods. Mulligan refused the order, stating it was against police regulations. The next night the same incident occurred with patrolman Daniel Bonjour. Both officers were ordered to appear before the Police Commissioners. They received warnings and the issue never arose again.[43]

Mayor Gleason continued to maintain his popularity with the working-class population of Long Island City, but the upper classes had always been embarrassed by his vulgarity, crudity, and his flagrant patronage, so they united to defeat him in the 1892 election. When the election took place, Gleason's corrupt administration weighed heavily against him and the local newspaper, the "Star", printed a devastating account of his misdeeds and his bullying, abrasive personality. Gleason's own treasurer, Frederick Bleckwenn, attacked him during the campaign. As a result, he lost to another Democratic candidate, Horatio S. Sanford, in a three-cornered election: Sanford tallied 2679, Gleason 2495, and Manly, the Republican, 1483. Gleason boldly challenged the vote by claiming that 1191 ballots had Sanford's name misspelled and that they should be voided.

Gleason's City Clerk Burke obligingly refused to certify Sanford's election; Sanford submitted his case against Burke to the Grand Jury. During this election turmoil Gleason had not forgotten about his distaste for Captain Woods. A rumor spread quickly that the Police Commissioners were getting ready to suspend Captain Woods and appoint Sergeant Thomas Darcy as acting captain. On December 27, 1892, the Commissioners transferred Darcy from the Hunter's Point Station House to Astoria and Sergeant Roulette from Astoria to Hunter's Point. Most members of the police department thought the moves were the first step in dumping the Captain.[44]

Gleason continued to contest the election, and to everyone's amazement, Gleason contrived to be seated as a grand juror and refused to heed the court's objection that he could hardly with propriety sit on a case in which he was vitally interested. The presiding judge put an end to the farce by ruling that Gleason was not able to serve. Gleason, nevertheless, refused to vacate the mayoral offices, barricading himself inside.

The new Mayor appointed new Police Commissioners, and Captain Woods appeared before these Sanford appointed Commissioners and said he would not obey either the Gleason or Sanford Boards until the courts settled the matter. Until that time, Woods said he intended to continue to perform his duties to the best of his ability without recognizing any superior officer.[45]

When the court finally declared Sanford to be the legitimate Mayor, Captain Woods was given the assignment to eject Gleason from his office. The low- key Woods showed no outward emotion with the ejection, but inside he must have been overjoyed with his opportunity to exact retribution.[46]

Captain Woods tenure under Mayor Sanford progressed without controversy, but he did suffer a personal tragedy. Arthur Woods, the youngest son of the Captain had sustained a foot injury in which gangrene had developed. On July 16, 1894, Arthur's foot was amputated by surgeons at St. John's Hospital. The operation was a success.[47]

The Sanford administration was a very quiet time for Captain Woods, at least as far as his job was concerned. Only one police controversy developed during the term, and it was extremely minor in nature compared to the incidents involving Mayor Gleason.

On June 2, 1895, forty policemen marched in a Decoration Day Parade. Each of the former Union states had adopted a Decoration Day by 1890 as a day to honor the American soldiers killed in the Civil War . As time went on, "Memorial Day" began to supplant "Decoration Day" as the name of the holiday, and it soon became a day to honor all fallen American troops, not just those from the Civil War.

The broiling sun, dusty roads and hard pavement were very trying on the marching officers. After the parade was viewed at City Hall by Mayor Sanford, the march continued up Vernon Avenue to Astoria. Captain Woods, who was a Civil War veteran, was himself fatigued as the parade reached Harris Avenue. He halted the procession of policemen and told them they could quench their thirst with water. The exhausted policemen went straight to Joseph Buschman's saloon, followed by the German band. For fifteen minutes Buschman and his assistants dispensed a miscellaneous assortment of beverages that did not include water. After several kegs of beer had run dry, Buschman began to make inquiries about payment. As the musicians gulped down beer after beer Bandmaster Raab assured Buschman that it was alright because the city would pay. The policemen became puzzled when asked to settle their bill and repeated the band's assertion that the city would take care of it. Buschman waited several days and received no money. Finally, he had to call Captain Woods and go before the Police Commissioners who reluctantly paid the tab.[48]

Everything seemed to be going well for Captain Woods. Even though he had always been in command of the police department he had his official title changed to Chief of Police. It was smooth sailing for Woods until the next election for Mayor.[49]

Paddy Gleason was back. The former Mayor still enjoyed support from working-class Irish people, many of whom longed for his paternalistic rule and Gleason was determined to vindicate himself by running again for Mayor.

In the election of November 1895 Gleason ran as a Democrat and his supporters showed their support of Gleason by putting axes in their windows. In a three-way election, Gleason scored his last personal triumph with 2550 votes. John P. Madden, the Jeffersonian Democratic nominee, had come incredibly close with 2520. Gleason's first act was to fire all the appointees of ex- Mayor Sanford. Gleason did not fire Captain Woods. That would have been too easy on the Captain. On January 3, 1896, Gleason sent a written order to Woods directing him to report to City Hall at 9 AM the next morning with a written answer to his order.

The big mayor frowned when Captain Woods entered his office, and the frown deepened to a scowl when the Captain handed him the sheet of paper containing the answer to his written order.

Without stopping to look at the paper, Gleason began giving orders to Woods. "I want you to appoint Cameron court officer in place of Reidy."

"I won't obey any orders you give me," Woods replied. "I am responsible only to the Board of Police Commissioners. Any orders I may receive from them I will obey."

"I don't want you to talk back to me," growled Gleason.

"I will talk back in reply to anything said to me," Woods responded.

Gleason became white with rage and ordered Woods out of his office.

"I'll go readily enough," Woods said.

"I'll attend to your case later," Gleason said.

"And I'll attend to yours," Woods nodded.

"You better go home to bed and sleep," sneered the mayor.

"I'll do that too, if I feel like it," Woods said as he departed.

Mayor Gleason then read the written document Captain Woods had handed him. Gleason's written order had directed the Captain to report to City Hall every morning at 9 AM for orders, and to be on duty from that time until midnight.

The written answer stated that Woods knew of no law which made him responsible to the Mayor, and if he was shown to be mistaken, he would obey the Mayor's orders. Until then he would only obey the Police Commissioners.

With this letter in mind, Gleason appointed William Fitzgibbons, John Grady, and John Lawlor as Police Commissioners – Commissioners who would be loyal to him.[50]

On the day he took office, Paddy "Battle Ax" Gleason marched through the streets of Long Island City like a triumphant Roman Emperor. The joyous throng of well-wishers not only followed the march, but they continued to follow the Mayor into City Hall and into his office. When he was standing behind his desk facing the crowd packing his office, he took off his hat. Someone in the crowd called for three cheers, but only one was given.

"Hold on," called out the Mayor. "I'll tell you when to shout."

A policeman forced his way through the crowd to keep them quiet, but Gleason said he did not need any police today. He said he was chief and declared he would preserve order.

Gleason stood on his chair and said, "I read in the newspapers that I was to be received here today with more dignity and ceremony than had ever been accorded a newly elected mayor of this city. I find that Mr. Sanford is not present and feel that some citizen should introduce me to the people of this city."

This was greeted with several rounds of applause. Gleason continued the speech that likely sent a chill down Captain Woods spine and made his blood boil at the same time as he stood in the corner of the office.

"Three years ago this month," Gleason began, "this office was entered by a gang of the worst ruffians, murderers and thieves, with Police Captain Woods at their head. They called upon each other to murder me, throw me out of the window, and to do other things. Revolvers were pointed at my head and insulting remarks made about my nationality."

After thanking all his supporters Gleason continued with his previous theme. "Three years ago, I was mayor of this city, and no law in the State of New York could depose me. City Hall was besieged." Gleason pointed to the corner of the office where Captain Woods was posted. "Three years ago I was ejected from this building by a gang of thieves, murders, robbers, and pirates, at the head of whom was that gray-headed old scoundrel . He committed an assault upon me. I was his benefactor. For three years he was out in the cold until I put him back at the head of the force. We have some police officers on the force of whom I am proud, while there are others that cause me to blush with shame. There are burglars, geese stealers, murderers, and pirates; policemen who hold citizens up against lampposts and rob them. I am chief now."

"Woods will be out in the cold soon," interrupted a hoarse voice, and cheers followed.

Captain Woods knew full well his days were numbered.[51]

After one month in office Mayor Gleason had ravaged the police department. Twenty-two patrolmen who had been appointed during the three years of Mayor Sanford's administration were dismissed and Captain Woods official title of chief was reduced back to captain. Gleason maintained that the appointments of the dismissed officers were not in accordance with the law. Captain Woods commented that the police department was in a state of demoralization.[52]

Mayor Gleason continued his assault on Captain Woods a month later when his Police Commissioners met to hear charges preferred against Woods. The specifications included general incompetency, neglect of duty, disobedience of orders, and ignorance of the police manual.[53]

Captain Woods had no intention of rolling over to the mayor's assault. To the contrary, he went on the offensive, filing a $50,000 lawsuit against Gleason for slandering him during his City Hall speech.[54]

The day after he filed his lawsuit, Captain Woods was suspended and Sergeant Darcy appointed acting captain.[55] His trial dragged on for months without a resolution. In the meantime, it took a jury only thirty minutes to award Captain Woods $5,000 in his slander lawsuit against Mayor Gleason.[56]

Gleason appealed the verdict, and the following month the judge ordered a new trial. In shifting back to the long, drawn-out trial of Captain Woods, the Mayor fired a new shot at the Captain when a new charge was entered against him. Woods had been under suspension for ten months when Philip Coffey, the Mayor's private secretary, observed Captain Woods use a pass to ride on the New York and Queens County Railway. The pass was only authorized for active police officers, not those under suspension.[57]

Finally, after more than a year on suspension the trial of Captain Woods concluded with the Police Commissioner's notifying him that he was dismissed from the force.[58]

The new trial in the slander lawsuit was slow to begin because Mayor Gleason claimed illness on several occasions as the trial was set to start. Finally, on January 4, 1899, the trial concluded with an award of $4,500 for Captain Woods.[59] By this time Gleason was now the ex-mayor of Long Island City because on January 1, 1898 Long Island City had been consolidated into the Greater City of New York.

Four months passed and Gleason had not paid the $4,500 judgement against him. Gleason was notified that a warrant had been issued and he would have to go to jail if the judgement was not paid.

"I am in need of a rest," said Gleason, "but even if I was not, I would not pay that judgement. A dark cell would have no terrors for me, but I will not have to remain in a cell. The jail limits now are larger than New York City and Brooklyn combined. It is the largest jail in the world, and it will not be a hardship for me to keep within its bounds." [60]

The judgement was reduced to $2,500, but Gleason was true to his word and was arrested on May 15, 1899. [61] Before feeling to sorry for the plight of Paddy Gleason, one needs to understand the significance of his statement where he said, "it is the largest jail in the world and it will not be a hardship for me to keep within its bounds." Gleason was not just indicating that he would be placed in a larger cell. Gleason was placed in the custody of the Sheriff of Queens County and confined to jail limits. In anticipation of being confined, the wily Gleason had a bill passed in the Legislature extending the jail limits to cover the entire county of Queens. Since all of Queens was considered part of the jail system, he was able to travel about the county as usual, to occupy his summer cottage at Arverne, and in fact, to do just about anything he pleased as long as he stayed in Queens.[62]

After serving the required six months within the "jail limits," Gleason was released. He was informed that the despite his imprisonment the judgement against him would stand for twenty years. After being released, Gleason embarked on a trip to Manhattan to see if he could notice any improvements in the six months he was forced to stay in Queens.[63]

Paddy Gleason may have thought he had won the final victory with his six month sentence in Queens, but Captain Woods was not done by a long shot. A few weeks after completing his six-month sentence Gleason was called to testify in a hearing to see if he owned enough property to satisfy the $2,500 judgement.

If anyone expected the questioning regarding Gleason's assets to be easy, they were sorely mistaken. Louis J. Grant represented Captain Woods and conducted the examination of Gleason.

Grant: Who owns the diamond shirt stud you have in your shirt front.

Gleason: It belongs to me.

Grant: (pointing to the diamond studded battle ax on Gleason's shirt.) And the battle ax?

Gleason: That's mine.

Grant: It's your battle ax, but I guess it's pretty dull since consolidation knocked you out?

Gleason: No, it's not dull, but it is as sharp as it ever was.

Grant: How many horses do you own, Mr. Gleason?

Gleason: I do not own any.

Grant: You own that famous team, Parnell and Gladstone, do you not?

Gleason: No, sir.

Grant: What became of them?

Gleason: I sold Gladstone eight years ago, and Parnell several years ago.

Grant: What horse did you drive up with this morning?

Gleason: Parnell.

Grant: Ahem! You did, did you. Then where did you get Parnell to drive?

Gleason: In the stable, corner of Front and Third Street.

Grant: Who gave you permission to use that horse?

Gleason: The Woodside Water Company, which owns him.

Grant: Who in the company gave you permission?

Gleason: Mr. Edward M. Tyrrell, the president.

Grant: How much did you sell Parnell for?

Gleason: $50

Grant: Rather a low price for such a famous horse, was it not, Mr. Gleason?

Gleason: Horses are much cheaper now than they were.

Grant: Mr. Gleason, did you ever own any interest in the old City Hall in Long Island City?

Gleason: I might have at some time or other during my extensive real estate transactions.

Grant: Don't you know whether you did or did not?

Gleason: No, I would have to look through the records of all my extensive transactions before I would answer positively.

Grant: What pieces or parcels of land have you handled.

Gleason: Gleasonville, with 1,100 lots – Charletteville, which consisted of 600 lots – the Bown estate, a piece of property in Kansas City – 500 lots at Rockaway Beach, adjoining Edgemere – 50 lots on Webster Avenue in this city – the Buchanan Estate in Astoria, about 40 lots – four buildings on Jackson Avenue – The Centennial Hotel on Thompson Avenue in this city – three houses on Third Street in this city – 40 or 50 lots around Maspeth – 3 four-story buildings on Sixth Street in this city – a three-story factory on Magin Street in New York. I guess that's all.

Grant: Quite a number of transactions, was it not? Did you ever have anything to do with the Mantell Estate of Astoria?

Gleason: Oh yes, that was another. That was only 90 lots and I forgot it. Cultivate my memory and I can probably tell you more.

Grant: Did you ever know a man named Brossell?

Gleason: Yes.

Grant: Where does he reside?

Gleason: In heaven, I hope.

Grant: How did you come to lose your property at Rockaway?

Gleason: Mortgage foreclosed.

Grant: How much was it for?

Gleason: Forty-one thousand dollars.

Grant: What was the property worth, Mr. Gleason?

Gleason: About $140,000, if not more.

Grant: Do you ever play cards at night for money?

Gleason: Certainly, I do, and I lose lots of times

Grant: Where do you play the games?

Gleason: At the headquarters of the battle ax in Front Street.

At that moment an attorney names Burke appeared in the courtroom and announced that Gleason had filed a petition for bankruptcy in The United States Court in Brooklyn.

As he left the courthouse, Gleason commented that going through bankruptcy was a sad ending to his busy railroad and political life, but that he was still very young and would try to outlive his hard luck. Captain Woods was going to have a very tough time wresting any money from Paddy Gleason.[64]

But collecting the judgement from Gleason was only one front in Captain Woods' war. He won a major victory on the other front when he was restored to the position of captain in the consolidated New York City Police Department.

In today's NYPD there is a maximum age limit for uniformed members of the service. When an officer turns 63-years of age he/she must retire. Apparently, no such law existed in 1900 because Captain Woods was 72-years old when he was reinstated.

The seventy-fifth precinct was the name given to one of the old Long Island City Police precincts. At 6 PM on February 6, 1900, the night platoon of police officers stood in front of the precinct desk. Acting Captain Thomas Lynch read the order of the Police Board restoring Captain Woods to duty by order of the New York State Supreme Court and assigning him to the precinct. Lynch thanked the men for their attention to duty during his term in command and introduced Captain Woods as the new commanding officer. Woods said he expected the men to be policemen from the crowns of their heads to the soles of their feet, and that if they obeyed orders, that was all that would be asked of them. On the desk stood a floral horseshoe four feet high bearing the word "Welcome." It was a gift from the men.

The return of Captain Woods was accepted generally as an act of justice for an efficient police official. He was the first man appointed to the old Long Island City Police Department on May 3, 1871. He remained in command until relieved by a political Police Board on the grounds that there was not enough money to pay his salary. He was out for nearly four years and then restored by the first Gleason administration. Captain Woods ejected Gleason out of City Hall when he was holding out against Mayor-elect Sanford, and for that act he incurred Gleason's wrath. No sooner was Gleason re-elected Mayor than he began waging war upon Captain Woods, and he finally succeeded in having him dismissed from the force. Then Captain Woods began a suit against Gleason for slander resulting in a judgement for $2,500 against Gleason. Gleason had failed to pay a cent of the judgement and filed bankruptcy. Captain Woods was off duty for over three years and when restored to duty he received back pay in full plus interest.[65]

Captain Woods' advanced age must not have thrilled some in the higher ranks of the new NYPD. Captain Woods was forced to take a civil service examination, and on November 11, 1902, it was reported that he passed the exam.[66] Three days later, however, Captain Cooney arrived at the Seventy-Fifth Precinct to take command from Captain Woods, who was retired.[67]

Two weeks later Captain Woods celebrated his 50th wedding anniversary with his wife in their house on Pomeroy Street. During the celebration Captain Woods was asked how he felt about being retired by Police Commissioner Partridge. Woods said, "As I was a veteran of the Civil War I could have fought my retirement, but I thought I had enough of fighting and decided to accept the decision of the Police Commissioner. But I believe I could still do duty of necessary."[68]

Captain Woods was not done fighting. His nemesis, Paddy Gleason, had passed away in 1901, but the Captain was still trying to collect the $2,500 judgement from his daughter, who had made it her business to avoid being served legal papers.

On May 20th, 1904, Miss Jessie Gleason sat inside St. Mary's Church for a mass honoring the third anniversary of the death of her father, Patrick Gleason. Outside the church, James Fiesel appeared to be making friendly small talk with a waiting coach driver. It wasn't friendly small talk. Fiesel was an officer of the Surrogates Court and he had finally tracked down Jessie Gleason, who had successfully avoided him for over a year. There was a reason Fiesel had chosen the specific driver to befriend. When the mass ended Miss Gleason went straight to her coach and Fiesel offered assistance by opening the door. Miss Gleason thanked the smiling man holding the door and reflexively accepted the papers he presented in his outstretched hand. The papers were served.[69]

I could find no record indicating if Captain Woods ever collected all or part of the judgement. Captain Anthony S. Woods died in his home in Astoria on December 20th, 1916, at the age of 89. The story of the Long Island City Police is in a large part the story of Captain Woods.[70]

PATRICK JEROME GLEASON

CAPT. ANTHONY S. WOODS.

The Poolrooms by the ferries in Long Island City

Interior of Poolrooms

LONG ISLAND RAILROAD STATION.

This is the road adjacent to the LIRR that infuriated Mayor Gleason and led to his famous raid to tear down the railroad fences.

Long Island City cop on patrol by entrance to Manhattan ferries.

IN THE LINE OF DUTY:

It is always a tragedy when a police officer is killed in the line of duty. The Long Island City Police Department suffered one line of duty death during its 28-year existence. The details of this loss is another integral chapter in the story of the Long Island City Police Department.

On February 6, 1883 the wind whipping off the East River made the frigid18-degree temperature seem even colder. Patrick Casey was known around his Long Island City neighborhood and the post he patrolled on Borden Avenue near the ferry entrances as "Smiling Paddy," but he wasn't smiling on this evening as he approached the Comisky's home in Hunters Point. Casey had known the Comisky brothers for 18-years, but the combination of a bad cold, the frigid wind, and the somber occasion made smiling an impossibility for Casey. The Comisky's mother had died the day before and was being waked inside their home on this evening.

35-year old James Comisky greeted Casey at the front door.

"I'm sorry for your loss," Casey whispered in a raspy voice.

"Thanks Paddy," James nodded. "Come in and sit with me a while."

The body heat from the crowd of mourners in the house made the environment more comfortable as Casey and Jack Comisky took seats in the corner of the living room.

"Where's Dick?" Casey asked, referring to Jack's younger brother, Richard Comisky.

"He's asleep in the other room," Jack replied. "He's on duty tonight. You know how it is."

Indeed, Patrick Casey did know how it was. Both he and Dick Comisky were policemen with the Long Island City Police Department. For the next hour Casey and Jack Comisky talked about old times in Long Island City with his mother. Then with no warning, Casey made an odd statement. "Dick better leave me alone."

Jack had trouble understanding the raspy voice. "What did you say, Paddy?"

Casey's voice grew louder. "If he don't stop following me up I will fix him."

Jack slapped Casey's back. "Oh, come on, Paddy, don't talk like that. Dick has always been your friend. If there's a problem, you should talk to him at the precinct."

Casey stared at the floor as Jack probed further. "What exactly did Dick do to you?"

"He is following me up all the time and I want him to stop it."

"Well," Jack shrugged, "I don't know anything about that."

Patrick Casey stood up, expressed his sympathies again, and departed into the freezing night.

It might seem strange for Richard Comisky to be sleeping while his mother was waked, but it was a fact of life for most policemen in the 19th century. There was no special time off for a death in the family so Comisky worked his overnight shift, came home, mourned his mother and then tried to get some sleep before reporting back to the precinct.

Comisky had been with the Long Island City Police Department since 1877 and his official rank was Roundsman. A Roundsman was a supervisory rank between police officer and sergeant that was abolished early in the 20th century. On February 6, 1883, Roundsman Comisky was functioning as an acting sergeant. Casey had been a policeman since 1875, and it was rumored that he was jealous that his boyhood friend had advanced in rank with less time on the job.

A little more than a month later Comisky was still working the same overnight shift. Casey was working a shift that ended at 2 AM. At about 8 PM on March 10th Casey visited the office of Police Surgeon William Burnett which was located down the block from the precinct. Burnett was talking with a man, but he paused when Casey entered. "Good evening, Casey, sit down a moment."

After bidding his visitor good night, Dr. Burnett returned to Casey. After a few words the doctor cut Casey off. "You seem hoarse, Casey, what is the trouble? Have you got a cold?"

"I have a little cold," Casey admitted.

"Do you have any soreness in your chest or pain in your lungs?"

Casey shook his head. "No pain, but there is a little soreness in the chest a good deal of the time."

"Do you feel sick?" Dr. Burnett asked.

"No," Casey replied, "and I am not sure whether it would hurt me to stay on duty."

"What time do you go off duty?" Burnett asked.

"Two o'clock in the morning."

Casey never asked to be excused from duty, but Dr, Burnett got the feeling Casey was looking for him to say he should go home for the remainder of his shift.

"Well," the doctor began, "since you don't feel sick, and you don't appear to be very sick you can remain on duty until then." Dr. Burnett gave Casey a prescription for his cough, and he departed the office.

At approximately 10:00 PM Officer Casey patrolled his post, but stopped on the sidewalk outside the Hunter's Point saloon owned by his boyhood friend, Henry Sharkey. Sharkey had also been friends with the Comisky brothers for many years. Sharkey observed his friend through the saloon window and went outside to greet him. Very quickly, however, Casey turned the conversation toward Comisky. "Dick Comisky keeps following me around my beat." Casey alleged.

"I don't think Dick would do that," Sharkey replied.

"It's not just him," Casey insisted. "The Mayor and Police Commissioner McGee are following me too."

"Listen to yourself, Paddy," Sharkey said. "The Mayor and Commissioner would do no such thing."

"Listen to me, Henry," Casey pled, "I seen them twice on my beat."

"Come on, Paddy," Sharkey responded, "They live in Long Island City. Why would it be so strange to see them on your beat?"

"I know what I saw," Casey said as he departed along the sidewalk.

Approximately 45-minutes later Sharkey heard a knock on the door that opened to a hallway next to the saloon. Casey was at the door with a lady Sharkey did not recognize and asked for two brandies. Casey and his lady friend finished their drinks quickly, handed the empty glasses back to Sharkey and departed without any conversation.

The neighborhood was quiet early Sunday morning as Acting Sergeant Comisky supervised the precinct along with officers Jerimiah O'Conner and Edward O'Brien. The station house was a high stoop, two-story and basement private residence at the corner of East and Hunter's Point Avenues. The front parlor was used as the sergeant's office and the back parlor was an assembly room for the men.

Comisky's house was a very short distance from the station house and at approximately 10:30 AM he went home to have breakfast with his father and brother. Comisky finished his meal and returned to the precinct. Comisky settled in behind the big desk and read the newspaper. O'Conner was sitting next to Comisky at the desk while O'Brien sat with his feet up on a table behind the desk. At about 11:30 AM the attention of all three officers was drawn to the front door. Patrick Casey had entered the precinct.

O'Conner had been a police officer for seven years, but he had known Casey from the neighborhood for twenty years. O'Brien was a boyhood friend of Casey as well and had known Richard Comisky for thirteen years.

Casey was coughing heavily as he walked past the front desk. O'Brien chuckled and called out, "What's wrong Paddy, are you dying?"

Casey mumbled some unintelligible words and continued into the assembly room. The three officers in the front room continued their conversation until a few minutes later when Casey called out to O'Conner from the assembly room. "Jerry."

O'Conner stood but did not leave the desk area. Casey called again. "Jerry, can you come help me?"

O'Conner entered the assembly room and observed Casey holding his revolver over a table. "Can you fix this for me?" Casey asked.

O'Conner took hold of the gun, but didn't see what was wrong with it. He called for additional assistance. "Ed," he shouted, "can you lend a hand here?"

When Ed O'Brien took the gun in hand, he immediately noticed that there was a pin keeping the cylinder from turning properly, and he fixed it. "Here you go, Paddy," he said as he placed the revolver on the table.

Casey grabbed his revolver and loaded it while O'Conner returned to his position in the front room with Comisky while O'Brien remained in the assembly room.

O'Conner was reading the newspaper when Casey emerged from the assembly room. He walked up to the desk and addressed Comisky. "Why have you been following me around all these nights?" Casey asked.

Comisky said something about making sure he did his duty but O'Conner wasn't sure of his exact words. O'Conner was quite certain, however, of what Casey said next. O'Conner dropped the newspaper out of his hand when he heard Casey declare. "Well, I will kill you dead!"

Casey raised his revolver and before O'Conner could move, he fired a shot. The bullet hit Comisky under the eye. Blood spurted out and his head went back, but he remained seated upright in his chair. O'Conner sprung forward and O'Brien raced out of the assembly room to subdue Casey, removing the gun from his hand in the process.

"Jerry, go get the doctor, quick," O'Brien implored

O'Conner took off sprinting down the street. He was out of breath when he reached Dr. Burnett's office. "Dr. Burnett, come quick," he huffed, "Casey shot Sergeant Comisky."

In the assembly room of the station house, an exasperated Ed O'Brien couldn't believe what had just happened. "Paddy, what did you do that for?" he asked Casey.

"Is he dead?" Casey asked.

"He is" O'Brien nodded.

"Well, it is done," Casey sighed, "and it can't be helped."

When Dr. Burnett entered the station house, he saw Comisky still sitting motionless in his chair behind the desk. He quickly examined Comisky and felt for a pulse.

"Is he dead?" O'Conner asked.

Burnett nodded. "The poor fellow is gone."

Burnett then went into the assembly room where O'Brien was standing guard over Casey.

"Casey, why did you do that?" Burnett gasped.

Casey stared at the wall and stated very calmly, "That fellow had been following me around." He then turned his head and stared at Burnett. "I asked you for an excuse last night and you would not give it to me."

"That's a lie, Casey," Dr. Burnett shot back, "you did not ask me for an excuse." Burnett than turned to O'Conner, "Is he disarmed?"

"He is disarmed," O'Conner nodded.

A short time later Police Commissioner McGee entered the station house. The Commissioner paused for a few moments to gaze upon the dead body of Richard Comisky, still sitting upright behind the desk. He then entered the assembly room where Casey was being held.

"Why did you do this, Casey?" McGee asked.

Casey answered in a low measured tone, "I couldn't help it. That sergeant was following me around."

McGee turned to O'Brien. "Have you placed him under arrest?"

"Yes, sir," O'Brien replied.

"Take him right away to the county jail," McGee directed.

"Commissioner," Casey said, "the county jail is where I want to go, and I want you to go with me."

Word had spread quickly through the neighborhood of the shooting, and a crowd had formed outside the precinct calling out threats toward Casey. Before the crowd grew larger and more hostile, Police Officer O'Brien and Commissioner McGee escorted Casey to the county jail.

Casey was charged with murder, and at his trial the Mayor and Police Commissioner were actually called as witnesses and questioned as to whether they were following Casey.

POLICE COMMISSIONER JOSEPH MCGEE ,

Q. In the month of March last were you a Police Commissioner of Long Island City?

A. Yes sir.

Q. You know the defendant, Casey?

A. I know him, yes.

Q. As a Police Commissioner or otherwise, did you follow
the defendant around on his beat?

A. No, sir, I did not.

MAYOR GEORGE PETRY

Q. You are Mayor of the city?

A. Yes, sir.

Q. Do you know the defendant, Casey?

A. Yes sir.

Q. He was on the police force in March last?

A. Yes, sir.

Q. Did you on Saturday evening, the month of March, or
did you at any other time, follow the defendant, Casey, around
on his beat in this city, to see that he did his duty, or for any
other purpose?

A. I did not, sir.

Q. When did you assume the office of mayor?

A. I took my seat the 15th of January 1883.

Q. Commissioner McGee was one of the new commissioners, was he?

A. Yes, sir.

Q. There had been a change in the Police Board after the inauguration of your term of office.

A. Yes, sir.

Q. Did you know much personally about the duties performed by Casey - personally, of your own knowledge?

A. Nothing, any more than any other policeman on the force.

Q. Did you reside in the neighborhood upon his beat?

A. Yes, sir.

Q. Saw him frequently?

A. Yes, sir.

Q. Saw him on duty?

A. Yes, sir.

Q. Did you observe him frequently or otherwise?

A. Observe him?

Q. Yes, to see him I mean.

A. Oh, yes, I saw him frequently. He was principally on duty in the same ward where I live.

Q. Do you know anything about his being on duty drunk or anything of that kind?

A. I don't know anything about him being drunk that night.

Q. Do you know about his being drunk at other times?

A. I have known him to drink, yes.

Q. Did you consider him a common drunkard?

A. No, sir.

Since there was no question of the fact that Casey had shot Comisky, his entire defense rested on the concept that he was insane through the chronic use of alcohol. The key witness on his behalf was his wife.

Mrs. Maria Casey had been married to Patrick for 8-years. Her testimony at the trial was intended to bolster the defense that Casey was suffering from insanity induced through alcoholism. Maria said she knew Casey about five years before they were married and that he was always a hard drinking man. She said they were periods of time when he was not drinking that he was kind and gentle towards her. But when he was drinking, he would be abusive and do strange things, such as insisting that Maria wasn't his wife and that the children were not his children. On several occasions she said he came home and asked for supper, and after eating the meal he demanded supper, insisting that he had not been given the food. On another occasion Maria said Casey sat in his uniform just staring at his wife. She asked if he was going to work, and he said he was leaving soon. Casey kept on silently staring at his wife until she asked "What in the world are you watching me for? What makes you be looking at me!" He did not answer, and Maria continued, "Ain't it time for you to go on duty?" and he says, "Yes, I guess so. " and he walked out.

Maria Casey also testified about a time he fired his gun in their home. She said he came home one day in a very excited state and said something that she could not hear. Maria said the next thing she remembered was the sound of the gunshot and a bullet whizzing past her head. She could not swear that he tried to point the gun at her when the shot fired, but that Casey immediately walked out of the house and went to his mother's nearby house. Casey's mother told Maria that Casey told her he was going to kill his wife and then himself.

Casey's first trial ended in a hung jury when one juror held out and refused to vote for conviction.[71]

Casey was convicted of murder at the second trial and sentenced to hang. His lawyer appealed the verdict, however and he was granted a third trial. The jury in the final trial reached a verdict on June 21st,

1883. The jury deliberated for three hours before returning to the courtroom at 8:30 PM. Casey looked nervous and excited when they entered the court. He held his youngest daughter in his lap and gazed intently on the twelve men who were to decide his fate.

County Clerk Sutphin spoke to the jury foreman. "What do you find, gentlemen?"

"Guilty of murder in the second degree."

Casey kissed his child, then his mother and wife. Judge Bartlett sentenced him to Sing Sing Prison for life.[72]

Patrick Casey had been an inmate under a death sentence, but the third trial resulted in a life sentence. On the day Casey had been sentenced to death a white dove flew into the courtroom and landed on his shoulder. The dove refused to move and accompanied Casey back to his cell and became his constant companion. At the same time, Charles Rugg, a notorious murderer, was also an inmate in the jail, awaiting trial for the murder of a woman and her daughter. On the day before his trial was to begin Rugg escaped, but two days later was captured and returned to jail. The day of his capture was the day of Casey's removal to Sing Sing to begin serving his life term. After being taken from his cell and while in the sheriff's office being prepared for his journey, Rugg was led in by his capturers. All this time the dove had been perched on Casey's shoulder, but as soon as Rugg was led in the dove flew from Casey's shoulder and over to Rugg, alighting on his shoulder, cooing as if it had found a long-lost friend.

All efforts on the part of Casey to call it back were in vain, and as Rugg was led back to the cell from which he escaped the dove went with him. It remained with him up to the morning of his execution. On that morning as Rugg marched up the scaffold the dove was perched on his shoulder and remained there until the black cap was drawn over his face. As soon as that was done the dove flew out one of the jail windows and was never seen around the jail again.[73]

With a life sentence to serve it was believed that like the dove, Casey would never be seen again in Long Island City. But unlike the dove, Casey returned. After serving 25-years Casey became the benefactor of a law that required the indeterminate sentence of life to be set at a fixed period of time. Casey was released on September 12th, 1907 and brought back to Long Island City by his nephew, William Lynch, where a celebration was waiting for him in his old home. His wife was there along with his three daughters, two with husbands and grandchildren. Casey was hale and hearty, not showing his age of 55. He commented that there seemed to have been a lot of changes for the better since he left Long Island City.[74]

The subject matter in this series of books has thus far involved mostly cops in the 19th century. A theme that has figured prominently into all areas of life during that period is alcohol. The vast majority of the crimes I write about as well as the cases of police misconduct had alcohol as a common denominator. When Patrick Casey tried to use insanity brought on through alcohol as a defense to murdering his supervisor, it caused me to pause and ponder a question. What the heck was going on with all the drinking in the 19th century? Were we a country of drunks, and is that what ultimately led to Prohibition?

History, by and large, tends to be considerably more complicated than our pop cultural understanding of it. A historical movement as broad as the prohibition of alcohol in the United States, for instance, was the result of so much more than a mere crusade of moralistic teetotalers. Just as it's grossly, hilariously simplistic to describe a conflict such as the Civil War as having been fought "to end slavery," it's equally myopic to think about a topic as complex as Prohibition in the terms of "drinkers vs. non-drinkers." In reality, there were so many other racial, political, religious, economic and nationalistic factors in play that the full story is actually an unlikely coming-together of many groups with very disparate goals, held in a bizarre alliance by their opposition to the alcohol industry.

With all of that said, though, there's one aspect of the road to Prohibition that is undeniable, and that's the American appetite for alcohol. In short: Some may consider Americans to be huge consumers of alcohol, but by today's standards, average alcohol consumption in large parts of the 19th century U.S.A. was almost beyond rational belief. I was finding it hard to accept as a fact just how much booze the average American was consuming in the first half of the 1800's. The figures are almost cartoonishly high. But then I paused to consider this current series of books I am writing. This is the fourth book in a series about obsolete police departments that operated within New York City. The common thread running through these agencies was that they all operated during the late 19th century. In performing my research, I discovered that the vast majority of the arrests made as well as the disciplinary actions taken against police officers were alcohol related. It seemed as if drinking was an accepted part of a policeman's life. This premise was summed up best by a captain's assessment of a police officer during the 1880s; "He's a fine officer when he's sober." So, how did we reach a point in the 19th century where alcohol was so much an American way of life?

Americans have always liked a drink; a trait that was initially brought over by hard-drinking European settlers. By 1770, Americans consumed alcohol routinely with every meal. Many people began the day with an 'eye opener' and closed it with a nightcap. People of all ages drank, including toddlers, who finished off the heavily sugared portion at the bottom of a parent's mug of rum toddy. Each person consumed about three and a half gallons of alcohol per year. We're talking about 3.5 gallons of pure ethanol, rather than gallons of a specific spirit. To convert that into a more graspable figure, that's 8.75 gallons of standard, 80-proof liquor per year for the average person by the time of the American revolution. That's already 45 percent higher than current consumption levels, but hold onto your seats, because the number gets much higher by the 1800s.

A number of factors led to an explosion of alcohol consumption in the early 1800s. First, the British halted their participation in the American molasses/rum trade, objecting to its connections with slavery, while the federal government also began to tax rum in the 1790s. At the same time, the settlement of the so-called "corn belt" in the Midwest created large new supplies of corn, which was cheaper and more profitable to convert into whiskey than it was to transport great distances without spoiling. Thus, western farmers could make no profit shipping corn overland to eastern markets, so they distilled corn into 'liquid assets.' By the 1820s, whiskey sold for twenty-five cents a gallon, making it cheaper than beer, wine, coffee, tea, or milk." In short, whiskey was extremely cheap and extremely available, and American consumption soared as a result.

Even the English, no slouches in terms of consumption themselves, noticed how sloppy their American cousins were getting. In English traveler Frederick Marryat's, *A Diary in America*, published in 1837, the writer remarks that the Americans seemingly drank for every conceivable occasion:

"I am sure the Americans can fix nothing without a drink. If you meet, you drink; if you part, you drink; if you make acquaintance, you drink; if you close a bargain you drink; they quarrel in their drink, and they make it up with a drink. They drink because it is hot; they drink because it is cold. If successful in elections, they drink and rejoice; if not, they drink and swear; they begin to drink early in the morning, they leave off late at night; they commence it early in life, and they continue it, until they soon drop into the grave." – Frederick Marryat

By 1830, alcohol consumption reached its peak at a truly outlandish 7 gallons of ethanol a year per capita. As if it really needs saying, 7 gallons of ethanol per year, per capita, is an insane number. Consider this: If a couple today were drinking at 1830 levels, they would be plowing through roughly 3.4 standard, 750 ml bottles of Jim Beam White Label Bourbon per week, in a single household. Their livers would be sending every conceivable manner of distress signal, assuming they didn't immediately shut down. Knowing this, it becomes much more understandable that this is when the temperance movement (which would eventually become the Prohibition movement) first began to coalesce and gain steam.[75]

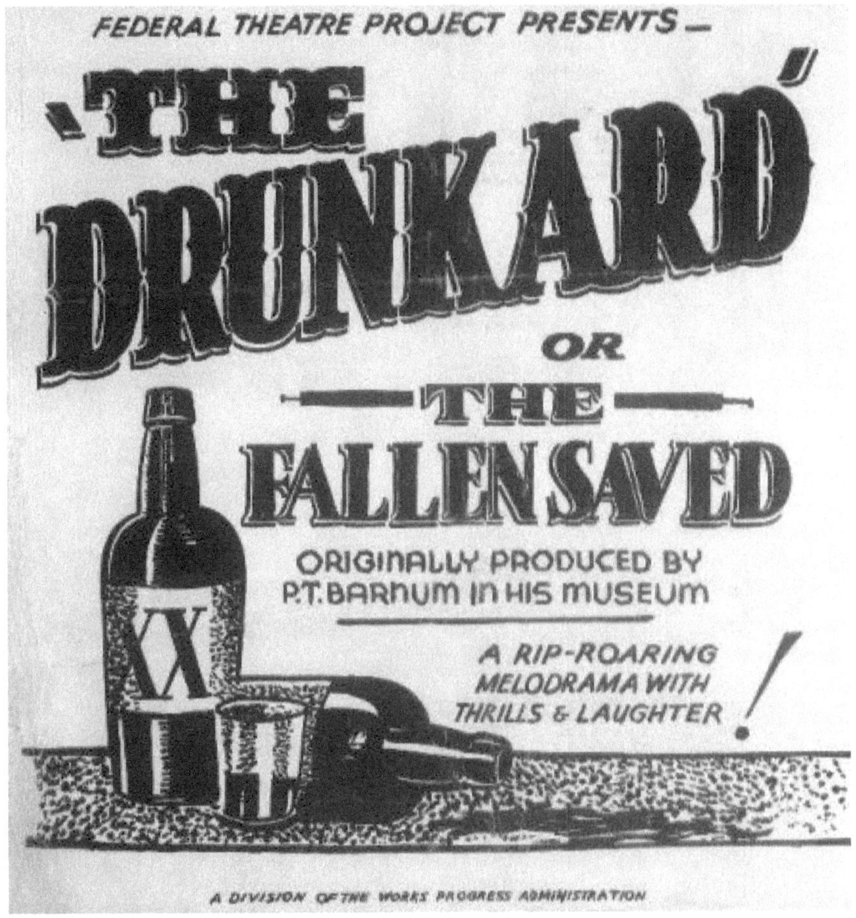

With the propensity of drinking in the 1800s, this was the
Most popular play of the period.

LONG ISLAND RAIL ROAD FE
34th STREET
JAMES

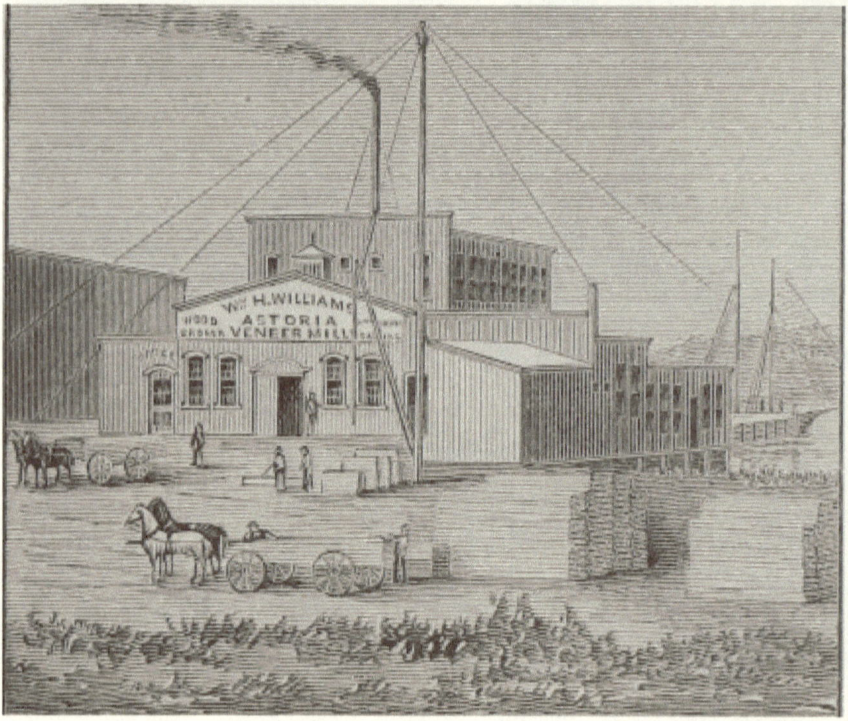

THE DEPARTMENT AT WORK:

The first report of a police action I could find was performed on July 20th, 1872, by Long Island City Policeman Paul Heaney, and it was controversial. On this Saturday night Heaney was patrolling his beat in Ravenswood when he was attracted to the movements of a drunken man in the street. When Officer Heaney got closer to the drunk, he recognized him as John Farmer.

Farmer grabbed hold of Heaney, saying, "Come have a drink with me."

Heaney refused and Farmer began to pull him around, tearing some of the buttons off Heaney's waistcoat. Heaney became excited and pushed Farmer away, telling him he would arrest him if he didn't move on. Farmer became enraged and began attacking Heaney. Heaney tried to arrest Farmer, but he resisted and was joined by some friends who tried to prevent the arrest.

Heaney said that it turned out Farmer was not very drunk because he was able to evade capture and run away at a faster speed than Heaney. When he realized he was not going to catch up with Farmer, Heaney fired his pistol in the air. Farmer was about to jump a fence with Heaney close behind him. Just then some stones thrown by Farmer's friends landed near the officer. The close proximity of the stones caused Heaney to discharge his pistol by accident, with the ball entering Farmer's back and lodging in his left lung.

Farmer's description of the incident differed from Heaney's in almost every respect. He said he did not try to escape from Heaney, was friendly with him, and good-naturedly took hold of him after asking him to drink. He also said that no stones were thrown.[76]

Public opinion in the case was against Heaney. It was believed to have been an outburst of private malice originating from a quarrel between Heaney's brother and the wounded man. Two witnesses stated that Farmer was in Solomon B. Noble's yard when Heaney fired the warning shot. They said Farmer then returned to Heaney, but when he came near enough Heaney grabbed at his head. The witnesses continued that Farmer was able to avoid the grab and dodged away at which time Heaney yelled, "If you run, I'll shoot you!" Farmer ran away and Heaney fired. Farmer continued to run until he reached a cornfield where he fell from exhaustion. A minute later Heaney arrived, and Farmer said, "Have mercy on me, I'm shot." He was placed in an old jolting wagon and driven to the station house.[77]

Officer Heaney was subsequently arrested and charged with assault with the attempt to kill. He was exonerated of the charges and returned to duty by the Police Commissioners.[78]

The 19th century Long Island Railroad police force was mainly a compilation of constables, special officers and watchman. Long Island Railroad Freight Agent Howard Smith was both relieved and upset. A bundle of clothing should have arrived in Long Island City from Jamaica on Thursday, but the clothes were missing. On Saturday evening, with the aid of Watchman Patrick Taft they found the bundle of missing clothing. That was the relief. Smith was upset when he discovered some of the clothes to be missing.[79]

Patrick Taft and Dennis Ryer were both Watchmen employed by the Long Island Railroad at the Long Island City Yard. They had worked overnights together for about 18-months. On Monday night at about 10 PM Ryer entered the depot office. The office was a small structure located about two blocks north of the passenger terminal, on Ferry Street. It was about fifteen feet square with a closely boarded partition, five feet high, dividing one corner from the remainder of the room. Inside the office was a stationary desk, a safe, a stool, and a large armchair. Taft was already sitting in the office and said, "Good evening, Governor."

The two watchmen talked about politics for about thirty minutes. Walsh, the watchman about to go off duty entered the office and suggested that the three of them go for a drink. Ryer was hesitant, not because he was on duty, but because he did not know how the medicine he was taking would react with alcohol. Taft urged Ryer to come along, so the trio went to the barroom in the nearby Long Island City Hotel. They drank for about an hour when Ryer leaned in close to Taft and said, "Pat, let's go to our work."

Taft insisted on another drink, the fifth since they entered. The conversation continued about politics and Boss Tweed in New York. Three men entered the barroom and announced they were looking for the watchmen in the depot and certain way bills. Ryer answered the man, but the conversation turned argumentative with Ryer removing his coat in preparation of a fight. Cooler heads prevailed as Walsh played peacemaker and the incident ended with a handshake.

Walsh boarded upstairs in the hotel, and he said goodnight and went to bed. Taft and Ryer proceeded to the depot and entered their office at about 1 AM. As was his habit Ryer laid his pistol on the table in the office. He said that since they arrived so late, he needed to immediately take a walk around the area. Taft told Ryer he was being too conscientious for the wages they were being paid, and that no one would touch anything in the yard. Ryer drew his attention to a box of groceries that were recently removed from a car, but Taft said he never heard about the incident. They continued talking in the office and Taft asked Ryer what time he went off duty the prior morning. When Ryer said 8 AM Taft asked why he stayed so late. Ryer said he wanted to see that all the cars were locked before he left the yard. The conversation then turned to a rumored reduction in wages and Taft said he wouldn't work for reduced pay. Ryer said he knew the hours were long, but he still had to pay for a roof over his head. Then the conversation began that lit the fuse.

"Pat, how did Smith make out with that clothing?" Ryer asked.

"I don't know," Taft shook his head, "I guess he put the someplace."

Whether Ryer was making a joke or an accusation was unclear, but his next statement was, "I partly guess they are some of the clothes you were trying on."

"That's a damn lie!" Taft yelled as he jumped up from his chair and made a grab for the pistol on the table. Ryer's hand reached the pistol at the same time and the two watchmen struggled for the gun. The pistol went off, but the struggle continued. The pistol went off a second time and Taft sank to the floor by a chair.

Taft extended his hand and said, "I forgive you, don't expose me."

What was Taft worried about? He had told Ryer that when he was helping Smith search for the missing clothes, he had found the clothes outside of Smith's presence and had tried on some coats but didn't take them because they didn't fit. That revelation may account for why Taft reacted the way he did to Ryer's statement.

Ryer asked, "Pat, what shall I do for you?"

Taft smiled, "Don't leave me."

Taft died a few seconds later. Ryer remained in the office for about fifteen minutes. He then went to a car to retrieve his lantern and walked with his dog to the lower end of the yard. There he sat considering what he should do. He went to the yardmaster's office but said nothing to the engineer. Ryer returned to the office to ensure Taft was dead, and then went home to tell his wife who told Ryer to immediately give himself up. Ryer found Long Island City Police Officer Minnocks and told him he had important information for Captain Woods. They traveled to the station house where Ryer surrendered to Woods.

The veracity of this story must be tempered with the understating that it was Ryer's account of what happened.[80]

At 7:05 AM Dell Carter, a clerk in the office, arrived and was surprised to find the office door unlocked. He went inside, assuming a watchman was inside, but when he didn't find anyone he went out to the street and bought some tobacco before returning to the office. When Carter still found no one upon his return he passed through a door leading to the yard at the rear and got a broom, with the intention of sweeping the office. As he opened the door leading into the little office in the corner of the room he saw Taft lying on the floor, and supposing he was asleep, turned to sweep out the other part of the building. He stopped, however, and returned to Taft to wake him. He called him three times and then grabbed him by the shoulder discovering Taft was dead.

When Carter notified the police, Captain Woods had just dispatched seven policemen to search for the murderer when Dennis Ryer surrendered himself. Captain Woods found Ryer's story of an accidental shooting suspect, especially when an examination of the office found evidence of three shots. Ryer was locked up in the First Precinct station house in Astoria to await the result of the coroner's inquest.

Ryer was described as being a big, burley fellow, with a red beard who was fifty years of age. He was known to completely terrorize employees of a smaller stature on the LIRR premises. He had worked for the railroad for twelve years. Taft had worked for the railroad for seven years and had never been known to carry a pistol.[81]

Dennis Ryer stood trial for murder, and the District Attorney claimed the incident was a clear case of cold-blooded murder. He detailed how Ryer placed the pistol on the table and quarreled with Taft. He said it was the height of absurdity to believe that during the scuffle Taft was accidentally shot – twice. The D.A. also pointed out that after the 3 AM shooting Ryer stood calmly by and saw his victim die. He said it spoke volumes that Ryer did not immediately report the shooting. Instead, he kept watch at the freight office until he left the office, went home and ate a hearty breakfast. Then, at 8 AM, after talking it over with his wife, Ryer finally surrendered himself to the police.

Ex-judge Busteed, defending Ryer, claimed the shooting was a pure accident and citing several factors to bolster the accidental nature of the shooting. He said that Taft and Ryer had been on good terms, and that Ryer once had sunstroke that he never recovered from. He stated that the whiskey drunk that night had excited both men unduly. Busteed said that Ryer voluntarily surrendered himself after consulting with his wife and that the pistol used in the shooting had originally belonged to Taft.[82]

On April 13th, 1877, the jury retired to deliberate the fate of Dennis Ryer at 2:15 PM and returned at 3:45 PM with the verdict – Not Guilty![83]

Probably the most notable crime in the history of Long Island City, was the Masked Burglary of 1876. A gang of dock thieves, half a dozen or more in number, led by one John James, crossed the East River from New York in a rowboat early on a Saturday morning to commit bold crimes in Ravenswood and Astoria. Six men, all masked with torn pieces of women's wrapper went to the Sunswick House, owned by Henry Green at the corner of Broadway and Vernon Avenue. With pistols in hand, they threatened the lives of the residents. and secured a large amount of goods, with which they safely escaped. While the Long Island City Police were looking for the perpetrators of the Sunswick House break-in, the crooks attacked the residence of Mr. Hiller, of Ravenswood, pillaging the premises of all valuables worth over $2,000.[84]

Miss Catherine Hiller was the first to encounter one of the burglars and they had this interesting dialogue when she stuck her head out of her bedroom door:

Burglar – Keep that head in there, Miss, or I'll knock it off.

Miss H. – Then I guess I'll take it in.

Burglar – That's a nice ring you've got on that dainty little finger. I want it.

Miss H. – You can't have it. If you live long enough, you will have a pair for your wrists.

Burglar – You're damn saucy, aren't you? Now, I'll take the ring and maybe a little piece of your finger.

He seized her for the purpose of taking the ring by force.

Miss H. – I will save you the trouble. Here it is.

She passed the ring over.

Then the burglar went to her writing desk and, finding it locked, broke a hole in the corner with the butt of his pistol.

Miss H. – Here, you stop that! Don't break anything in this room.

Burglar – Oh, you're opening your pretty mouth, are you?

This was addressed to Miss Hiller's sister, who was trembling for her life in the bed.

Miss H – Don't you interfere with her. I made that remark.

Then the keys were handed over and the desk and bureau drawers examined. Having collected the most valuable articles, the spokesman of the gang addressed Miss Miller.

Burglar – Is there anything else worth a fellow's while to take?

Miss H. – Yes. There's a picture and a clock; and there's a Bible. Take the Bible, and when you're not robbing you might find things in it to interest you.

Burglar – No thank you – goodbye.

Miss H. – You have taken everything valuable in the house, why don't you complete the job by setting it on fire?

Burglar – If it's an accommodation to you, I would just as soon fire it as not. It won't take a minute.

He ignited a match for that purpose.

Miss H. – Never mind, sir. [85]

Ever since the burglaries occurred the Long Island City Police were working hard at trying to find the crooks, or at least some clues, but they were unsuccessful until the Tuesday after the crimes. A man told Long Island City Patrolman Maher that he had information about the crimes. Officer Maher had heard the man talking about the burglaries, so he grilled the man as to his knowledge. The man, whose name was kept confidential, said that two days after the burglaries he met a man named John Connors who resided in South Brooklyn. During a conversation Connors said he was part of the burglary gang. He detailed how his gang of six men landed in Astoria with a boat and after robbing the homes rowed back to Brooklyn.

Acting on the information, Maher informed Chief Campbell, of the Brooklyn City Police, and told him he wanted to arrest John Connors, and requested assistance from the Brooklyn Police. The Chief sent him at once to Captain Leavy at the Third Precinct, and he detailed Detective Mahoney to hunt down Connors. In less than 24-hours Mahoney arrested Connors and locked him up in the Third Precinct. Chief Campbell telegraphed Officer Maher to come and take his prisoner. Captain Leavy was not certain that the description of the informant matched Connors, so he telegraphed Maher and told him to bring the informant, and that he would only release Connors if the informant positively identified him. Officers Maher and Lang brought the informant to the Third Precinct where he failed to make a positive identification. Connors was subsequently released from custody.

With the crooks still at large Chief Campbell detailed Detectives Zundt and Looney to the case, and they were relentless in their pursuit of the culprits despite being treated in an inhospitable manner by Captain Woods. Woods must have resented the involvement of the Brooklyn City Police, as he refused to aid them or to divulge important information. The Captain received much public criticism, as it was felt he should have provided any assistance possible to bring the crooks to justice.[86]

The break in the case came on New Year's Day when Captain Murray, of the New York Police, received information to the effect that some of the robbers were hiding in the city. In an action that Captain Woods must not have been too thrilled about, New York and Brooklyn detectives rounded up the entire gang. John James and five others were indicted, tried, found guilty and sentenced to jail. James received 35 years, the others 15 years.[87]

Police officers in New York City are provided a pass to ride the Long Island Railroad free of charge. The free ride is not a courtesy for cops, it is done to draw more cops to use the railroad and to be available to take police action should it become necessary. Taking an off-duty police action is not a modern phenomenon. Back in 1877 New York Police Captain McCullagh had an interesting incident while riding the railroad with his family into Long Island City.

McCullagh was returning from Rockaway to Hunter's Point, where he was spending the summer when a fight broke out on the train and several passengers asked him to break it up. How the passengers knew McCullagh was a police captain was unclear.

McCullagh and a few passengers attempted to stop the fight, but one of the combatants, Richard Conroy, a Long Island City politician, struck him in the face, even though McCullagh had displayed his police shield. The disturbance, which resulted in the stabbing of one man and the disfigurement of others was finally quelled, and at the Hunter's Point Ferry Captain McCullagh showed the result of the blow inflicted by Conroy to Patrolman Patrick Boyle, of the Long Island City Police, and asked him to arrest his assailant. Boyle, who was said to have been intoxicated, at first refused, and was rude, but was induced to go with Conroy and McCullagh to the Second Precinct Station House where McCullagh's witnesses were not given a hearing from Sergeant Carroll, but on the testimony of Conroy's gang, who were rough characters, their leader was discharged. Captain McCullagh took his action to his home turf, and the next day he received permission from the New York City Police Commissioners to follow up the case, and he swore out a warrant for Conroy's arrest and also made a complaint against the behavior of Officer Boyle to the Long Island City Police Commissioners.[88]

What may have been at least partially responsible for the poor attitude displayed by Patrolman Boyle was the state of Long Island City's finances. The police had not been paid for two months when the Captain McCullagh incident occurred, and four months later they had still not received their wages.[89]

Drinking wasn't the only vice running rampant during the 19th century. This was the age of Tammany Hall and Boss Tweed. Political corruption was a way of life in Manhattan and Long Island City was a microcosm of its neighbor across the river and corruption in the city government was as bad, if not worse. The politicians weren't the only ones lining their pockets. In 1880 a couple of Long Island City Police Officers got into the act.

John Kavanagh was the only detective on the force and John Lang had been detailed by the Police Board to act as clerk in the Recorder's Court, and clerk to the Sanitary Inspector, Dr. Taylor.

There were residents of Long Island City who raised pigs and cattle on their farms and to feed them they utilized the services of "piggeries." Piggeries were establishments engaged in the business of boiling swill to be fed to cattle and swine. Piggeries were not businesses that could be licensed, so the mostly German owners of these locations operated in a gray legal area. Most of the time the city authorities turned their heads from their activities unless a location was creating a large health hazard that was generating numerous complaints. This type of questionably legal business was ripe for the workings of two corrupt cops looking to exploit the new immigrant community.

Lang would receive the complaints received in the Sanitary Department regarding piggeries, but instead of forwarding the complaints to Dr. Taylor, he would keep them himself. Lang and Kavanagh would travel to the piggery in the complaint under the guise of enforcing the law. Lang would inform the proprietor that his place had been complained of, and unless he paid $50 for a license, they would be compelled to tear down his shanties, destroy his boiler and close out his business. The price was, in every instance, regarded as too high, but the officers were obliging enough to reduce it to suit the size of a man's purse, sometimes taking as little as $5. The most they received from any one person was $22.50, but in every instance they exacted the promise of more. The license the proprietors received consisted of a permit to keep a certain number of horses, cows, pigs, and poultry, and it bore the name of Dr. Taylor as Sanitary Inspector, and John Lang as clerk or Deputy Inspector.

Dr. Taylor declared his name was a forgery and that he never inspected these piggeries, and that consequently they had never been condemned. Not only did the rogue cops extort money from the proprietors, but they also terrorized a woman. Mrs. Nable alleged that they seized her physically, showed her the handcuffs and threatened to take her to jail in their wagon. Her husband wasn't home, but Lang and Kavanagh didn't believe her, and under the pretense of searching the house for him, threw everything about and upset a bed and clothes closet. Mrs. Nable had, some time before, been almost murdered by a farm laborer and robbed of $70, so the effect of Kavanagh's and Lang's behavior was extremely upsetting to her, leaving her sick for several days. Mrs. Nable protested that she had no money, which was likely true. The officers gave her three days to raise $25, but she could only raise $9, and this, she alleged, she paid to Lang at his residence and took a receipt for it. He also gave her a permit.

When the actions of these officers came to light they were called before the Police Board. Lang admitted having received monies from the piggery proprietors. He tried to claim he had recorded the transactions properly, but in reality, he had not made any report of the transactions until the evening of this meeting, after he had received charges from Captain Woods.

The corporation Counsel advised the Police Board that there was no law permitting a piggery creating an illegal nuisance to be licensed and suggested that Lang be directed to refund to the parties all the monies obtained from them.

Lang and Kavanagh claimed they were acting under the authority of the Police Board, but the Board had no authority to direct the officers to perform the inspections and collect monies. Under very peculiar circumstances, several days after the board meeting a resolution suddenly appeared showing that it was introduced by Commissioner McNamara, directing an inspection of the piggeries by Sanitary Inspector Taylor, with a view to their abatement if found to be a nuisance. After Lang and Kavanagh were arrested, the prosecution claimed this resolution was fictitious, but regardless of its authenticity, it conferred no authority on Lang and Kavanagh to perform the inspections and collect money.

The politics of the period apparently came into play, as after their arrests, Lang and Kavanagh swore they would not become scapegoats and that if they went down, others were going down with them. Perhaps only one of the accused had the juice to make such a threat.[90]

John Lang was put on trial during July of 1881. The District Attorney chose to prosecute him only on the complaint lodged by Mrs. Nable. As previously recounted, Lang and Kavanagh visited Mrs. Nable's house where they demanded $25 from her for the privilege of keeping her pigs. Mrs. Nable said that the officers would have to deal with her husband, who was not home. Lang and Kavanagh then proceeded to enter the house to look for her husband, and in the process, they threw her beds out on the floor. Mr. Nable came home while they were inside the house and the officers made the same demand of money upon him. Both husband and wife swore there was no money to give, and Lang said that if the money was not paid in a week the pig pens and sheds would be torn down.

William Nable, the husband, testified that Lang told him he must have the money in two days or he would close his place up. Mr. Nable said he went to Lang's house, paid him $9 and took a receipt. Lang told Mr. Nable he would take a little less than $25 because he felt bad for the trouble his family had experienced. Lang was evidently referencing the time a farm laborer robbed the Nable's of $200 and nearly killed Mrs. Nable in an assault.

Dr. W.R. Taylor, Sanitary Inspector, testified that he never appointed John Lang a deputy inspector and never had authorized Lang to sign his name. Six other witnesses testified that Lang and Kavanagh had attempted to shake them down for money in the same manner as the Nable's had been treated.

John Lang took the witness stand in his own defense and tried to claim that he had been authorized to take the money for permits and to negotiate the amount of the fee. Under cross examination, however, the District Attorney shredded his story, and it took the jury a very short time to return with a guilty verdict. Land was sentenced to nine months in prison.

But wait a minute, what happened to Detective Kavanagh? It seemed that the detective may have been the one who had the juice to make the threat about taking everyone else down with him. Or perhaps it was something much more obvious.[91]

Lang had been discharged shortly after he and Kavanagh had been arrested in June of 1880. Lang was subsequently tried and convicted, but where was Kavanagh? Kavanagh was advised to resign and then he would have the opportunity to clear his name. It seemed like the only thing required to clear his name was to do nothing and wait for people to forget. On December 2, 1885, a very small article in the Brooklyn Daily Eagle read as follows:

The Grand Jury of Queens County, on different dates indicted Daniel Brunz, of Newtown, for burglary; Edward Eastment, of Glen Cove, for embezzling school funds, and Owen Kavanagh, of Long Island City, for blackmail while a member of the police force. Yesterday, in the Court of Sessions, Judge Armstrong ordered a nolle prosequi to be entered in each case.

Nolle Prosequi means the decision was made not to prosecute and the case was dismissed.[92]

What about Kavanagh? Did he come back on the job? Kavanagh applied for reinstatement to several different Police Boards but failed until 1892 when he was reinstated as a patrolman. How could he have gotten reinstated after resigning for his part in a blackmail scheme? I found a newspaper article from 1893 that verified he was still a Long Island City Police Detective, and more importantly, it may explain Kavanaghs immunity from prosecution and discipline.

On May 28th, 1893, at 10:30 PM, Patrick Downey, a watchman for the Long Island Railroad was on duty at the railroad offices on Front Street. John Rooney and Michael Hanley approached him and complained that they had just been assaulted by Detective Kavanagh of the Long Island City Police. While the two men were making their complaint, Kavanagh arrived on the scene and began attacking Downey, knocking him down with a blow to the head with an umbrella. When Downey fell, Kavanagh attempted to hit him again, but Downey reached up and grabbed the umbrella. Kavanagh let go of the umbrella and pulled out his blackjack. With this he hit the prostrate man several times. Downey was able to get up and stagger into the cashier's room, a few feet away. Kavanagh followed him and dealt him a terrific blow to the head, knocking him senseless. A judge was passing by and heard the commotion. The judge told Kavanagh to take the battered Downey to the station house and lock him up. Why would the judge direct that Downey be arrested when all he knew was that he had been beaten to a pulp? Well, the Judge's name was Kavanagh, and he was Detective Kavanagh's brother. Are there any more questions as to why only Lang took the fall in the blackmail case?[93]

Kavanagh soon learned that politics swung both ways when he fell into disfavor with Mayor Gleason. In one of the Mayor's last official duties before the consolidation of the City of Greater New York, Kavanagh was dismissed from the force under the premise that he had been illegally reappointed to the force without passing a civil service examination.[94] Kavanagh fought a legal battle for reinstatement and eventually was reinstated to the New York City Police Department on March 18, 1899.[95]

Things were looking up for Kavanagh again, and he was made a detective again and detailed to the office of the Queens District Attorney. Once again, Kavanagh became the victim of political fallout in 1900. District Attorney Merrill's Office raided a saloon in Long Island City operated by Patrick McCarthy. Merrill had information that there were many illegal activities taking place inside this house of ill repute and that the police knew about it and did nothing. Therefore, Merrill did not tell Kavanagh of the raid until it was about to happen. When NYPD Chief Devery found out that the District Attorney had conducted the raid without notifying his department, he was incensed and immediately transferred Kavanagh and another detective out of the DA's office to patrol duties.

For the next decade Kavanagh bounced around administrative assignments in Queens until he passed away while still on active duty on September 18, 1911, at the age of 62.[96]

Three years before the Richard Comisky tragedy, there was another cop on cop incident with much less severe results, but once again, drinking figured into the equation.

On August 27, 1880, Roundsman Corrigan was on patrol checking on the patrolmen on their beats. He was having trouble locating Patrolman Ayres, but eventually found him in a saloon under the influence. When Corrigan began to address Ayres condition, the patrolman lit a cigar, smiled, and threw a few choice insults at Corrigan before departing the saloon.

The Roundsman returned to the station house to notify the sergeant that he was charging Ayres with drunkenness, but when he arrived, he found Ayres already inside the precinct. When the smiling Ayres spied Corrigan, he immediately continued his barrage of insults, which so angered the Roundsman that he lost his temper and knocked Ayres down, injuring him to the extent that he had to go on the sick list.

Besides the charges against Ayres, Captain Woods also had to charge Corrigan for his physical attack on Ayres. Corrigan said he realized he was wrong, but that he had reached his boiling point with Ayres who had been doing anything he liked and boasting that his father-in-law, City Treasurer Morris, had influence to keep him on the force.

I could not find a record of the result of this hearing, but there were articles that substantiated that both Ayres and Corrigan were still members of the Long Island City Police Department long after this incident.[97]

It can't be overstated how much politics, and in many instances corrupt politics, played a role in late 19th century government in Long Island City. Anyone who has watched professional wrestling knows the "sport" is a never-ending struggle of good guys vs. villains, and on a regular basis these wrestlers change roles, with the good guy turning evil and the bad guy suddenly developing a conscience. Mayor Gleason was anything but a champion for clean government, but every now and then, even if it was for his own selfish reasons – he became a good guy.

Long Island City Justice Delahanty had long been considered a judge of questionable scruples, as he was known to enforce the law against certain criminals and to look the other way with those he favored. Mayor Gleason had a similar philosophy, but when their loyalties clashed, someone was going to have to assume the role of the good guy. In this battle between Gleason and Delahanty it was the Mayor who became the good guy.

Delahanty had been using his influence to protect the operations of an illegal gambling saloon in Blissville, and in particular, one of the operators named George Lucas.

On Saturday evening, August 27, 1887, Long Island City Police Officer Thomas Harty was enjoying a quiet evening inside the station house filling in for the shift as the sergeant. It wasn't going to remain a quiet evening much longer.

Fresh from the raid at the Blissville saloon, a squad of policemen entered the station house with George Lucas in custody. The sergeant leading the raid informed Officer Harty that Justice Gleason had determined that Lucas was not eligible for bail. That's correct, I said "Justice Gleason." In a very controversial move the Mayor also managed to have himself appointed as a Police Justice in Long Island City. The sergeant and the rest of the squad departed the station house, but before leaving, the sergeant told Officer Harty that no bail should be afforded to Lucas without the express authorization of Justice Gleason.

A short time later an irate Justice Delahanty burst into the station house and ordered Harty to produce the prisoner so he could set bail. Officer Harty refused, stating that he had orders from his superior officer stating otherwise.

The next day a captain from the Queens County Police arrived at the home of officer Harty. I'll admit I'm a little hazy on the "Queens County Police." I found several references to such an agency, but nothing regarding their origin or structure. I believe they were the police agency that covered the areas of Queens that did not have their own police departments. Anyway, the captain arrived at Harty's home and served him with an arrest warrant for contempt for disobeying the order of Justice Delahanty. He was taken into custody while in uniform to serve five days and pay a $25 fine.

By the time Harty was brought before Justice Delahanty, attorney Walter C. Foster had arrived to represent Harty. When Justice Delahanty took his seat, he immediately called out, "Is Thomas Harty in court?"

Foster stood up and said he was representing Harty. The Court Clerk read the charge of contempt and ordered Harty to stand. The clerk then asked Harty, "What have you to say to this charge?"

Foster jumped in. "As far as the warrant is concerned, I demand the immediate discharge of the accused on the ground that the court has no jurisdiction. I desire a ruling on that."

"Overruled," Delahanty sneered, "I simply want to know what Mr. Harty has to say to purge himself of this contempt."

"I have nothing to say," replied Harty.

"You have no apology to offer this court," said Delahanty.

"I desire to say...," Foster began.

"Mr. Foster," interrupted Delahanty, "you keep quiet. I am talking to Harty."

"Do you refuse to listen to me?" asked Foster.

"I do," nodded Delahanty. "I want Harty to answer me directly."

The question was repeated to Harty who again stated he had nothing to say.

"If that is the case, then," said Delahanty, "I will adjudge you guilty of contempt and fine you $25 and five days in the county jail."

"I desire to say this to the court," Foster chimed in. "That I want placed on the record that I objected to the court acting in this matter on the ground that he had no jurisdiction and that I desired an examination but was not allowed to speak."

Delahanty told Foster he was too late because he had already passed judgement on the case.

"Alright, then," Foster said, turning to Harty. "Harty, you go to jail, and I will get a writ of habeas corpus and have you out soon."

"Harty," Delahanty barked, "will go to jail when I make out a commitment for him. I am presiding here this morning and not Judge Gleason or Judge Foster."

When Harty was released after serving his five-day sentence he was still wearing his police uniform. He was whisked to City Hall where Mayor Gleason gave him a hero's welcome and took him through the streets in an impromptu parade.

Captain Woods and the Police Commissioners commended Officer Harty for obeying orders, even under the most extreme circumstances.[98]

Have you ever received one of those ridiculous email scams where someone has chosen you to spilt a multi-million dollar fortune with them, but they only need you to front the money for some fee to release the funds. You may wonder who would ever fall for these con jobs, but it happens all the time. These scams are also not new. Back in 1888, the Long Island City Police had to attempt to alert the citizenry not to fall victim to these frauds.

At that time the many villages on Long Island were worked by one of the most barefaced swindlers on record. His method was clumsy and preyed on simple minded people. The authorities in Long Island City received a letter from Mr. Townsend Albertson, of Albertson, Long Island, containing a circular. Mr. Albertson said the circular was received by a poor man named George Appleby, who lived near him, and that the circular was obviously a confidence swindle. The circular read:

Mr. George Appleby:

DEAR SIR: Over $2,000,000 of the great estate of the Hon. W. Vanderbilt were left secretly, to be given to the poor, regardless of race or color, in proportions of $50 each

Send an agent $3.50 within ten days and five days thereafter you will receive $50. This is only to help the poor of the State of New York as far as it will go.

The $3.50 you send to the agent helps to pay the Executive Board only. You will do well to send in your order at once, for we wish to close the estate as soon as possible.

Be careful to send your full address to

PO Box J.L. CHURCH, Agent, Long Island City

The envelope in which the circular was contained was mailed from Brooklyn, and the address was written in a plain but rough handwriting. The circular was printed but the figures contained in it were filled in with ink. Captain Woods took charge of the letter.

Postmaster James McKenna told Captain Woods that this scam had been working in Philadelphia a while back and had now obviously made its way to New York. Over one hundred years later these cons are still going strong all over the world.[99]

As the 1897 calendar ran out, there were many moist eyes in Brooklyn as their city faded into the annals of history and became just a borough in the Greater City of New York. There were no such regrets in Long Island City where the people had voted almost unanimously in favor of the consolidation. Real estate would boom in Long Island City after the consolidation, and everyone would reap the benefits.

Seven months later, however, the story was much different. The people were no longer as enthusiastic about the consolidation. The many benefits they believed they would derive had failed to materialize. Real estate, instead of booming, as was predicted, was in a down market. Property owners were alarmed over the prospects of higher and ruinous taxes, and the great public improvements promised had not come about. If another vote was taken in July of 1898, it would likely yield as many votes against the consolidation as there had been for the merger.

Long Island City had voted almost as a unit for consolidation, for the citizens honestly believed there would be a mad rush of capitalists from Manhattan and Brooklyn to buy their vacant lots that constituted so large a portion of the area of the city which for many years had the distinction, if not the honor, of having more politics to the square inch than any other municipality in the country had to the square foot. Governor Cornell once declared that Long Island City gave him more trouble than all the rest of the State of New York.

It is said that every cloud has a silver lining, and the silver lining in Long Island City was the reconstruction of the Police Department offered through consolidation. For years the department was in a deplorable state. The police were the subservient tools of the mayor in power, and the power of the mayor was absolute. The charter which

William Tweed gave to Long Island City invested the mayor with the authority of a Police Justice, and if the Mayor wished to commit some oppressive act against a citizen and was doubtful whether the Police Justices could be relied upon to do his bidding, he could exercise his prerogative as a committing magistrate and have the offending, and generally unoffending citizen, hauled before him.

The Long Island City Police department was always demoralized. A policeman who did not have pull with higher ups was a creature to be pitied. The old-time state of affairs passed away with consolidation, leaving a Long Island City police force that was disciplined, courteous to citizens, and effective in performing their police duties. After becoming a part of the New York City Police Department, the men felt that if they did their duty they would be protected by their superior officers, and they were no longer in a state of terror that the "boss" in power may persecute them without cause.

The citizens of Long Island City were unanimous in their praise of the police force, which as part of the NYPD came under the direction of Deputy Chief Elias P. Clayton and Inspector Nicholas Brooks. In Long Island City, the new 75th Precinct in Hunter's Point was placed under the command of Acting Captain Thomas H. Lynch, formerly of the Greenpoint Police Station, at Manhattan and Greenpoint Avenues. Captain Thomas F. Darcy, a veteran on the Long Island City police force was put in command of the 74th Precinct in Astoria.

The final recap of the manpower of the Long Island City Police Department on December 31, 1897 was 1 captain, 8 sergeants, 9 roundsmen, 66 patrolmen, and 1 electrician.

The two precincts in Long Island City were renamed the 74th and 75th Precincts. When representatives from the consolidated NYPD visited the precincts, they described the condition of the precincts as follows:

Seventy-fourth Precinct—This station is in fair condition. The interior requires pointing up and painting; front door and vestibule requires painting and graining; inside blinds require repairing; ten new lights of glass are required; roof needs repairs; plumbing in basement requires a general overhauling; the heating apparatus is insufficient to heat the building; many of the doors and locks are out of order; the prison needs repairing; cell doors and locks arc out or order.

Seventy-fifth Precinct—This station house is in a bad condition, being unsafe, unsanitary, totally inadequate and unfit in every particular. There are no sleeping-rooms for the Captain, Sergeants or Roundsmen, and they are compelled to rent rooms at the expense of the city.

In 1903, plans for a new 75th Precinct station house on the north side of 4th Street, 100-feet west of Vernon Avenue were approved, and the building was completed in 1905. In 1908 the precinct was renamed the 275th Precinct and in 1918 it became the 59th Precinct. Finally, in 1929 it became the 108th Precinct, the designation that remains today.

Today's 108th Precinct station house is the same building from 1905, just a few years after the Long Island City Police Department was consolidated into the NYPD. The officers assigned to the 1-0-8 should be aware of the history of their precinct and should give credit to the men who paved the way for their modern-day careers serving the citizens of Long Island City.[100]

CAPT. ANTHONY S. WOODS' OLD POLICE STATION AT ASTORIA, 1871.

1905 photo outside the new 75th Precinct. This is the same building that houses today's 108th Precinct.

108th Precinct

Bibliography

1. Nevius, James, LONG ISLAND CITY'S FORGOTTEN HISTORY, 11/16/2018
2. MILITARY POLICE RULE, Brooklyn Times Union, 1/18/02, p13
3. FIFTY YEARS MARRIED, The Brooklyn Daily Eagle, 11/26/02, p6
4. MILITARY POLICE RULE, Brooklyn Times Union, 1/18/02, p13
5. A MISSING CHIEF OF POLICE, The Brooklyn Daily Eagle, 7/13/1872, p3
6. CONSTERNATION IN LONG ISLAND CITY, The Brooklyn Union, 7/13/1872, p2
7. WOODS, The Brooklyn Union, 7/15/1872, p2
8. POOL SELLING, The Brooklyn Daily Eagle, 6/16/1879, p1
9. A DANGEROUS CHARACTER, The Brooklyn Daily Eagle, 3/24/1880, p3
10. UNTITLED, The Brooklyn Daily Eagle, 5/23, 1880, p2
11. LONG ISLAND CITY'S POLICE FORCE, The New York Times, 1/19/1883, p8
12. POOL SELLING IN LONG ISLAND CITY, The New York Times, 5/3/1882, p9
13. POOL SELLING PROTECTED, The Brooklyn Daily Eagle, 5/8/1882, p4
14. POOL ROOMS RAIDED, The Brooklyn Daily Eagle, 7/3/1882, p4
15. LONG ISLAND CITY'S POOL-ROOMS, The New York Times, 7/4/1882, p5
16. POOL SELLING, The Brooklyn Daily Eagle, 7/10/1882, p3
17. AN OFFICIAL BUMPUS, The Brooklyn Daily Eagle, 7/10/1882, p3

18. LONG ISLAND CITY POOL ROOMS, Brooklyn Times Union, 7/21/1882, p1
19. THE POOL SELLERS MUST GO, Brooklyn Times Union, 7/27/1882, p4
20. RESULTED IN A FARCE, Brooklyn Times Union, 7/28/1882, p1
21. POOL SELLERS HOLDING THE FORT, The Brooklyn Daily Eagle, 7/29/1882, p4
22. POOL ROOMS IN LONG ISLAND CITY. The New York Times, 7/29/1882, p3
23. LONG ISLAND CITY POLICE, The New York Times, 8/25/1882, p9
24. THE POOL-SELLERS, Brooklyn Times Union, 9/28/1882, p1
25. THE POOL ROOMS MUST GO, The Brooklyn Daily Eagle, 10/5/1882, p4
26. LONG ISLAND CITY POOL ROOMS, The New York Times, 10/6/1882, p2
27. LONG ISLAND CITY'S POLICE FORCE, The New York Times, 2/1/1883, p5
28. UNTITLED, The Brooklyn Daily Eagle, 2/4/1883, p6
29. LONG ISLAND CITY's TROUBLE, The Brooklyn Daily Eagle, 2/18/1883, p6
30. UNTITLED, The Brooklyn Union, 5/13/1883, p1
31. UNTITLED, The Brooklyn Daily Eagle, 6/24/1883, p1
32. CAPTAIN WOODS CONTEMPT SUIT AGAINST THE LONG ISLAND CITY POLICE BOARD, The Brooklyn Union, 7/7/1884, p4
33. A LIVELY ROW, The Brooklyn Daily Eagle, 1/20/1885, p4
34. GUSSIE WERNER'S DISAPPEARANCE, The Brooklyn Daily Eagle, 7/20/1887, p4
35. THE MISSING SERVANT GIRL, The Brooklyn Daily

Eagle, 7/21/1887, p2

36. THE ROOSTERS SAY WELSOME, The Brooklyn Daily Eagle, 8/26/1887, p4

37. THE BLISSVILLE RAID, Brooklyn Times Union, 8/29/1887, p2

38. UNTITLES, The Brooklyn Daily eagle, 9/7/1887, p4

39. ARRESTING HIS OWN SON, The New York Times, 6/7/1888, p3

40. GLEASON DID IT, The Brooklyn Daily Eagle, 7/28/1888, p4

41. BAGGING THE GAMBLERS, The Brooklyn Daily Eagle, 3/31/1889, p20

42. EJECTED BY MAYOR GLEASON, The Brooklyn Daily Eagle, 4/2/1889, p6

43. INSUBORDINATION AMONG THE POLICE. The Brooklyn Daily Eagle, 8/22/1891, p3

44. POLICE TRANSFERS IN LONG ISLAND CITY, The Brooklyn Daily Eagle, 12/28/1892, p10

45. HORATIO S. SANFORD DECLARED MAYOR, The Brooklyn Daily Eagle, 1/17/1893, p12

46. SANFORD IS MAYOR, The Brooklyn Daily Eagle, 1/20/1893, p1

47. AMPUTATED HIS LEG, The Standard Union, 7/17/1894, p5

48. POLICEMEN IN TROUBLE, The Brooklyn Daily Eagle, 6/3/1895, p14

49. CHANGES IN THE POLICE FORCE, The Brooklyn Daily Eagle, 12/28/1895, p14

50. DEFIANCE FOR MAYOR GLEASON, The New York Times, 1/5/1896, p8

51. GLEASON MAYOR AGAIN, The New York Times, 1/10/1896, p8

52. CAPTAIN WOODS BOTHERED, The Brooklyn Daily Eagle, 2/1/1896, p14

53. CAPTAIN WOODS TRIAL, The Brooklyn Daily eagle, 3/10/1896, p5

54. FOR $50,000 DAMAGES, The Brooklyn Citizen, 3/13/1896, p1

55. CAPTAIN WOODS SUSPENDED, The Brooklyn Daily eagle, 3/13/1896, p5

56. GLEASON MUST PAY $5,000, The Brooklyn Daily Eagle, 10/17/1896, p14.

57. POLICE CAPTAIN WOODS' PASS, The Brooklyn Daily Eagle, 1/28/1897, p4

58. CAPTAIN WOODS DISCHARGED, The Brooklyn Daily Eagle, 6/10/1897, p4

59. VERDICT AGAINST GLEASON, The Brooklyn Citizen, 1/5/1899, p10

60. EX-MAYOR GLEASON READY TO GO TO JAIL, The Brooklyn Daily Eagle, 5/14/1899, p10

61. MAYOR GLEASON ARRESTED, The Brooklyn Citizen, 5/16/1899, p1

62. UNTITLED, The Brooklyn Citizen, 6/9/1899, p9

63. GLEASON FREE ONCE MORE, The Brooklyn Daily Eagle, 11/16/1899, p7

64. GLEASON'S AFFAIRS AIRED, The Brooklyn Daily Eagle, 12/17/1899, p12

65. CAPTAIN WOODS IN COMMAND, The Brooklyn Daily Eagle, 2/6/1900, p7

66. CAPTAIN WOODS RESTORED, The Brooklyn Daily Eagle, 11/11/1902, p10

67. UNTITLED, The Brooklyn Daily Eagle, 11/13/1902, p3

68. FIFTY YEARS MARRIED, The Brooklyn Daily Eagle, 11/26/1902, p6

69. PROCESS SERVER AS JEHU OUTWITTED MISS GLEASON, The Brooklyn Daily Eagle, 5/20/1904, p6

70. ANTHONY S. WOODS, The Brooklyn Citizen, 12/21/1916, p2

71. THE ONE OBSTINATE JUROR, The Brooklyn Daily Eagle, 4/25/1883, p4

72. VERDICT IN THE CASEY TRIAL, The Brooklyn Daily Eagle, 6/22/1884, p12

73. THE TALE OF A DOVE, The Colorado Weekly Chieftain, 11/1/1894, p8

74. LIFER RELEASED, The Brooklyn Citizen, 9/13/1907, p7

75. Vogel, Jim, The 1800s: When Americans Drank Whiskey like it was Water, 8/10/18

76. OFFICER HEANEY'S VICTIM, The Brooklyn Union, 7/22/1872, p4

77. UNTITLED, The Brooklyn Union, 7/23/1872, p2

78. LONG ISLAND CITY, The Brooklyn Union, 8/21/1872, p4

79. THE HUNTERS POINT SHOOTING CASE, The New York Times, 12/8/1876, p5

80. PATRICK TAFT"S DEATH, Brooklyn Times Union, 12/6/1876, p4

81. MURDER IN LONG ISLAND CITY, 11/28/1876, p8

82. THE TAFT HOMICIDE, The New York Times, 4/13/1877, p8

83. END OF THE TAFT HOMICIDE CASE, The New York Times, 4/13/1877, p10

84. UNMASKD, The Brooklyn Daily Eagle, 12/30/1876, p4

85. A PLUCKY YOUNG LADY, The Brooklyn Daily Eagle, 1/12/1877, p3

86. UNMASKD, The Brooklyn Daily Eagle, 12/30/1876, p4

87. THE MASKED BURGLARS, Brooklyn Times Union, 1/

5/1877, p4

88. NO SHOW IN LONG ISLAND CITY, Brooklyn Times Union, 7/24/1877, p4

89. UNTITLED, Kings County Rural Gazette, 11/24/1877, p4

90. SERIOUSLY ACCUSED, The Brooklyn Daily Eagle, 7/13/1880, p4

91. BLACKMAIL CHARGED, The Brooklyn Daily Eagle, 7/14/1881, p2

92. THE LAST THREE INDICTMENTS, The Brooklyn Daily Eagle, 12/2/1885, p4

93. A BLACK JACK, The Standard Union, 5/29/1893, p4

94. UNTITLED, The Brooklyn Daily Eagle, 11/28/1897, p21

95. POLICEMEN REINSTATED, Brooklyn Times Union, 3/18/1899, p9

96. OWEN J. KAVANAGH, The Brooklyn Daily Eagle, 9/19/1911, p10

97. POLICEMEN FIGHTING, The Brooklyn Daily Eagle, 8/28/1880, p4

98. SEE-SAW, Brooklyn Times Union, 8/30/1887, p1

99. A BARE-FACED SWINDLE, Brooklyn Times Union, 8/23/1888, p1

100.POLICE IMPROVEMENTS, Brooklyn Times Union, 7/29/1898, p9